SHAUNDILIA PHILLIPS

Silent Screams

First edition

ISBN: 979-8-218-93400-2

This book was professionally typeset on Reedsy.
Find out more at reedsy.com

This book is dedicated to my children.

Disclaimer

This story is drawn from real experiences. To protect the privacy of those involved, some names and identifying details have been changed. Portions of the narrative have been dramatized, and some dialogue is recreated from memory to the best of my knowledge. While every effort has been made to remain true to the events described, this book reflects my personal recollections and perspective.

Content Warning

This story contains portrayals of physical, mental, and verbal abuse. Some scenes explore the effects of manipulation, intimidation, and emotional harm. Please prioritize your well-being while reading.

Note To Readers

This book is a testimony of the pain I've endured, the silence I survived, and the grace that carried me through it all. Writing it brought tears to my eyes—tears for what I went through, but also for the strength I didn't know I had.

Through every dark moment, God was there. Even when I didn't feel Him, He was holding me together. Because of His mercy and unshakable love, I'm still here. A walking, breathing testimony of His grace.

Prologue

"No, STOP!"

A scream rang out from my parents' bedroom; it was my sister— I froze.

Because I knew that scream.

I had lived that scream.

Thinking back, It was the same silent scream I swallowed on the nights he came into my room. The nights he'd lift me from the bed I shared with my little sister, carrying me into the bed he shared with my mother. I always knew what was coming. I'd scream in my mind, tears streaming down my face, as his hands moved where they never should have. But no sound ever escaped. The fear choked it all down.

And every time it ended, he whispered the same haunting words:

"Don't tell your mother. It would kill her."

This trauma marked the beginning of pain that carried into my adulthood. Guilt and shame shaped my self-esteem, pushing me toward people-pleasing and away from recognizing my own worth. When I met Sam, who I believed was the love of my life, every emotion surfaced—both the good and the bad, and I wasn't prepared for what that would uncover.

1

Chapter 1

The Start

I saw my little sister burst into the living room, tears streaming down her face. "Don't let him touch me, don't let him touch me again," she kept saying over and over as she ran around the couch and leapt into my lap. That's when it hit me—he's been hurting her too. Not her. Not my baby sister. Not your own flesh and blood. I thought it was only me... because I wasn't your biological daughter. Afterward, you'd send me back to my room, and I'd tiptoe in, trying not to wake her—never knowing you'd been doing the same thing to her. Tears began to flow as I thought about it.

"Come here, Tiffany!" he shouted from the back room.

"No, no, no," she whispered, burying her face in my chest, clutching me like her life depended on it.

"Please, Punkin… don't let him get me."

I couldn't believe this was really happening. What do I do? I'd been silent my whole life—too scared to speak, swallowing my screams.

And now… he was coming.

He was tall, medium build, light-skinned—smooth talker. That's probably how he got my mother in the first place.

We heard his footsteps rounding the couch, getting closer. He stopped in front of us and stared. His eyes were terrifying—they were cold, dark, and lifeless.

"Come along, Tiffany. Now."

"Leave us alone," I said, my voice shaking but steady enough to carry weight. "Wait till Momma gets home."

His face went pale. His eyes lost focus, distant, hollow. He stood frozen—like he was watching his life flash before him.

We could see it: fear. All over his face. Even as he tried to act tough, tried to force his voice to be strong.

"Let me tell you girls something, you bet not—"

But he didn't finish.

The sound of keys at the front door cut him off.

"Marie," he said

My mother was a missionary, and people often said she was blessed by God— miracles seemed to follow her prayers. She was tall and medium-built, with milk chocolate skin and thick, coarse black hair that waved gently at her shoulders. But she always brushed it back into a ponytail and pinned it up neatly. She wore head coverings and long dresses or skirts, modest and graceful.

Religion wasn't just a part of her life—it was her foundation. She was raised in a home where church came before everything. My grandparents lived and breathed faith. All of her siblings were deeply involved in ministry—pastors, missionaries, musicians. Some played the organ or guitar, and nearly all of them could sing until the Spirit filled the room.

I remember her telling me the story of her birth. Right after she came into the world, her tiny body went stiff. Her breathing turned shallow, and her eyes rolled back and forth. She was born at home, in a small white wooden house resting on brick stacks with a tin roof, out in the country.

The midwife was there, along with four of my grandmother's youngest children. They all stood silently, watching this beautiful, brown-skinned baby girl lying limp in my grandmother's arms, her life slipping away.

Then my grandmother noticed a copy of the Good News Paper—a church newsletter filled with testimonies and miracles. It was lying on the bed. She laid my mother on top of it and cried out to God.

"Save my child, oh Lord! Cover her with the blood of Jesus. Send your healing power right NOW!"

And in that moment, something happened. My mother stretched her little arms out as if in praise, turned her head, looked around, and kicked her legs. Then she let out the softest, sweetest cry.

I believe that day she was touched by God, anointed from birth. But nothing could have prepared her for the trials that would soon test her faith.

All eyes were locked on the front door—it felt like it opened in slow motion. My stepdad looked at us, then back at the door, as if he knew this might be the moment everything unraveled.

My mom walked in, singing one of her favorite hymns: "I know the Lord will make a way, oh yes He will."

She smiled. "What are you girls still doing up?"

She was glowing, still riding the spiritual high from the tent revival. But in an instant, that peace shattered. My sister jumped from my lap and ran to her, tears streaming down her face. She wrapped herself around our mother's waist, clinging tightly and refusing to let go.

"What's wrong, baby?"

I sat frozen, tears falling, whispering "Mama" over and over. The words wouldn't come. I was too afraid. I was afraid she'd hate me, blame me, think I let this happen.

She looked at my stepdad. "What's going on?"

He took a step back, fumbling for words. "You know how dramatic these girls are."

"Mama," I finally managed, curling into myself on the couch, "he's been doing things to us."

"What did you say, Punkin?"

I lifted my head. "He's been doing stuff to me... I didn't want to... I'm sorry.

I'm sorry."

My mom stood frozen, shock written across her face. Tears welled and spilled over, mascara streaking down her cheeks in dark lines. She turned to him, her voice barely steady. "Is this true, John?"

She gently pulled my sister from her waist and began walking toward him slowly. My sister ran back to the couch, grabbed my arm, and held tight.

"Now, wait a minute, Marie," he stammered, edging toward the back of the house. "You can't believe anything that girl says."

That's when she saw the knife on the table—next to the cake we'd been eating earlier.

Her eyes filled with fury. "So you've been touching my girls?" she said, picking it up.

Her eyes turned bloodshot with rage. The vein in her forehead pulsed. She thought of every bath he gave them, every quiet moment she wasn't watching—was he doing it then?

"Oh my God, my babies," she whispered, tears returning.

She stepped toward him, waving the knife. "I'LL KILL YOU!" she screamed.

She lunged—just grazed his arm as he spun and fled to the bathroom, slamming the door shut.

"You're crazy!" he yelled from the other side.

She pounded the door with her fists. "Open this door, you pervert! How could you do this to your own children?"

Then her body leaned into the door as she slid to the floor, crying out, "Why? Why?"

We walked over and sat beside her. She stared up at the ceiling, murmuring that question over and over. At first, I thought she meant him. But now, looking back at that moment, I believe she was talking to God.

We held her there for what felt like forever.

When the crying finally stopped and her prayers grew quiet, she looked at us through her tears, smiled faintly, and said, "Go put your shoes on."

As we laced up our shoes, I watched her steady herself, pressing against the bathroom door. She leaned in close and whispered something. I couldn't hear it all—but I caught the last part:

"May God have mercy on your soul."

Then she slammed her fist against the door.

We walked out of that old brown two-bedroom wood-frame house with the yellow trim, climbed into the car—and never looked back.

When my mom believed me, relief came first. It was quiet but overwhelming, like finally being able to breathe after holding everything inside for too long. But it didn't stay. Shame followed close behind, settling in my chest, and then fear. I started to worry about what would happen once the truth was no longer just ours—what people would say, how they would look at me. My mind filled with imagined scenes of judgment and whispers, of being teased, unloved, forgotten. In every version, I was alone, and that loneliness felt just as frightening as the truth itself.

2

Chapter 2

The Trip

As my sister and I sat in the backseat, holding each other and drifting off to sleep, I could hear our mother quietly crying to herself. Soft gospel music played on the radio, filling the silence. She began to sing along, her voice trembling:

"Walk with me, Lord, walk with me... while I'm on this tedious journey, I need Jesus every day to walk with me. Hold my hand, Lord... hold my hand..."

Then the song broke something in her, and she burst into tears again.

"Momma, are you okay?" I asked gently.

"I'll be alright, baby," she said, her voice barely holding together.

She turned down a bumpy dirt road lined with tall trees. The curves were sharp, and the absence of streetlights made the night feel eerie and endless. We drove for what felt like forever, until finally, we pulled into a driveway bordered by large stone rocks. It led up to a house tucked deep off the road.

As we got closer, I saw it: a red house with white trim around the windows and a wide front porch, complete with a white swing. The sight stirred something in me—familiarity.

I nudged my sister. "Tiffany, wake up. We're at Big Momma and Grandpa's house."

The car's headlights illuminated the front windows as we crept up the drive. The house looked dark, still, and cold. I glanced at Mom, who was wiping away the black streaks of mascara on her face and trying to smooth her hair with trembling fingers. She took a deep breath.

"You girls wait right here," she said softly, and stepped out of the car.

She stood on the porch for a long moment, frozen in place, as if second-guessing whether she should be bringing us here at all. She raised her hand to knock just as the porch light flicked on and her father's voice came from inside:

"Who is it?"

"It's me, Dad… it's Marie."

Relief washed over her face. She was grateful it was him who answered, not her mother.

The door opened. "Child, what are you doing here this late?" He looked past her. "You got those girls with you? Out this late at night? Y'all come on in."

9

He held the door wide. "Okay, Daddy," she said, and walked back to the car.

She turned off the engine and headlights. "Before we go in," she said, "I need you girls to be on your best behavior."

"Yes, ma'am," we answered together.

We followed her up the four wooden steps to the porch. Grandpa stood at the door with his arms stretched open, ready to welcome us. We knew what came next—his usual ritual. He hugged us, then placed a hand on each of our heads, clapped his other hand against it, and smiled like he always did. My sister and I exchanged confused glances. We never understood why he did that, but we figured it was just Grandpa's quirky way of showing love.

Inside, the house was cold, the floors creaking with every other step. As Mom led us to the back, we saw our grandmother standing in her bedroom doorway.

"Gracious alive, what are y'all doing here this time of night?" Big Momma asked, confused.

"It's good to see you too, Mother," Mom said softly, kissing her cheek. "Can we talk in the morning? I'm tired, and I really need to get the girls to bed. Good night, Mother."

"Good night, dear."

It felt comforting, lying in bed between my mother and sister. For a moment, I felt safe. Peaceful. Like I could finally rest.

But that peace didn't last.

Staring up at the ceiling, a deep unease settled in. Fear crept back into my chest. I knew Mom would want to talk about everything... and I wasn't ready.

Would she blame me?

Would she think I wanted it?

Would she still love me after she knew how long it had been going on?

Tears began to slip down my cheeks as I thought about all the times I could've said something but didn't—too afraid, too ashamed.

I closed my eyes and whispered a prayer into the darkness.

Lord, I'm scared. I don't know how to say this, and I don't even know where to start. I've kept this inside for so long, and I'm afraid that once I tell her, everything will change. I don't want my mom to look at me differently or stop loving me. I closed my eyes, but the tears still came. Please give me the strength to say it out loud. I don't think I can do this on my own.

3

Chapter 3

The Talk

"Wake up, Punkin, wake up! Big Momma made breakfast," Tiffany whispered as she shook me until my eyes fluttered open. Sunlight streamed through the curtains, casting a soft glow over the room like a warm kiss. The smell of salt pork bacon and homemade biscuits drifted through the air. I could already taste the maple syrup and melted butter she always drizzled on top. My mouth watered just thinking about it.

We made our way to the kitchen and saw Big Momma at the stove, scrambling eggs fresh from the henhouse out back.

"Sit down, girls—what y'all standing there for? Time to eat," she said, placing the eggs on the table beside a pot of creamy wheat cereal.

The table was overflowing with food. We didn't know where to start. I piled bacon into a biscuit, drenched it in syrup, took a bite—and oh my God, my mouth was in food heaven.

By the time I was halfway through my second plate, I looked and felt like a swollen pig. My eyes had been bigger than my stomach. I leaned back in my chair, content, until I heard voices down the hall.

"We need to go back over there and put a hurting on him for what he did to those girls."

"Hush, Amanda! The girls are in the kitchen—they'll hear you."

That was my mother's voice.

Curious, I gently pushed my chair away from the table and tiptoed down the hall, inching closer to the room where my mom and the other women were talking. I stopped just outside the doorway, careful not to be seen. I peeked in, trying to see who she was telling my secret to—the secret I had kept hidden out of shame, fear, and the belief that maybe she'd blame me or stop loving me.

The same fear that haunted me all night returned like a shadow creeping back in. I felt a sinking in my gut.

"You didn't suspect anything at all?" one of the women asked.

My mom looked down, her voice low and heavy. "Well, one time we were on vacation in Hot Springs. We took the girls swimming at the hotel pool. They were having a good time, laughing, playing... then John got in the pool."

She paused, visibly pained, eyes clouding with the memory.

"He said, 'I'm going to teach them how to swim.' I was sitting on a lounge chair putting on suntan lotion when I noticed the look on Punkin's face. He was holding her close, and the smile she had vanished. He stretched her out, legs straight so she could kick, moving her through the water. I couldn't really see where his hands were, but I couldn't stop staring at her face. She had this... hollow look."

She wiped a tear from her cheek.

"Later that evening, I asked her—just the two of us—if her dad made her feel uncomfortable. She told me no. Maybe I should've pushed it harder. But I believed her... because she said no."

I remembered that day like it was yesterday—summer of '88. That was the first time I ever lied to my mother.

Tiffany and I had been splashing around, laughing. Then he came. "Looking good... mighty fine, yes indeed," he whispered to me, eyeing me like I was grown, like I wasn't just a little girl.

The water was crystal clear. I saw his hand move to the front of his shorts before he came closer. My sister wandered to the other side of the pool, distracted with her Walkman.

He pulled me to him. I could feel it—hard and pressing against me. He pretended to help me swim, lifting me in the water, but his hands were somewhere else. Rubbing my legs, slipping between them, touching places no child should ever be touched.

I froze. My body stiffened. I wanted to scream, but I couldn't find the words. My mom was right there. Watching. I screamed in my head, begging her to save me—but nothing came out.

Why didn't I say something?

Tears welled up in my eyes at the memory, burning with guilt and helplessness.

"Punkin!" Big Momma's voice startled me, making me jump. I bumped into a small table, knocking over some pictures and her glass angel figurines.

"Come away from there! That's grown folks' business!" she scolded.

My mom turned and saw me—tears in my eyes. She looked heartbroken, maybe even embarrassed that I'd overheard.

I turned and ran down the hallway, past Big Momma, into the bedroom. I buried my face in the pillow, wishing all of it would just disappear.

A gentle knock came at the door.

"Can I come in?" my mom asked, her voice soft and steady.

"Yes, ma'am," I whispered, my face still turned to the wall, too afraid to look at her.

With each step she took, my heart pounded harder. I feared this was the moment she'd tell me she didn't love me anymore.

She sat down on the edge of the bed, silent for a moment, then reached over and touched my shoulder.

"Punkin, sit up for me, baby girl."

I turned slowly.

"We need to talk about what happened to you and your sister," she said gently. "But first, I want you to know something—no matter what... I love you. And there's nothing you or anybody else could ever do to change that."

Her words hit me like a wave. I stared at her, wide-eyed, tears spilling down my face.

"I love you," she said again.

I lunged into her arms, wrapped my arms around her waist, and buried my head in her chest.

"I'm sorry, Mama... I didn't want to... I promise," I sobbed, my words muffled.

"I know, baby... I know," she whispered, stroking my hair. She held me close and began to hum Amazing Grace. As she sang, her voice cracked, and tears ran down her face. She started praying in the Spirit, her voice trembling but strong.

I closed my eyes and prayed silently.

Asking God to take this hate from my heart... teach me how to love again, the way You do.

In that moment, the weight I'd carried for so long began to lift. I felt stronger—like maybe I really could face anything.

But I had no idea what was coming next.

4

Chapter 4

The Plan

"Are we almost there? I'm getting hungry," Tiffany said loudly, her voice cutting through the quiet hum of the Greyhound bus. I pulled the headphones off her ears and whispered, "You're loud... and no, I don't think so."

"Oh," she replied, slipping the headphones back on and flipping over the New Edition tape in her Walkman—the one Mom bought her earlier that day.

We were both growing restless. It had only been two hours, but it felt like forever. I turned toward the window, watching the blur of trees and small towns pass by, my mind drifting back to what I had overheard last night.

I had woken up in the middle of the night to get a drink of water when I noticed light spilling from the den. Curious, I crept down the hallway and heard my mom's voice—she was on the phone. I tiptoed back to the kitchen and picked up the other receiver as quietly as I could, holding my hand over it so she wouldn't hear the click.

"You did WHAT?" a woman's voice shouted on the other end.

"I went back to the house," my mom said, her voice shaking with fury. "I was looking for his gun. I wanted him to show up—I was going to blow his darn head off."

"Soon as he stepped foot through that front door," she continued. "But instead, I found a pawn ticket. He pawned it last week."

"Lucky bastard," the other woman said.

"Yeah... very," my mom replied, her tone still burning. "But I wasn't done. I grabbed the biggest kitchen knife I could find and sat down right in front of the door. I was boiling with rage. I sat there for almost three hours. He never came. I finally gave up and went back to my parents' house. Brenda, I just wanted him to feel what I was feeling."

"That's understandable," Brenda replied. "He's a low-down dirty dog who belongs six feet under. Nobody can blame you—not even your holy roller Christian friends."

"Girl, stop!" my mom said, a small laugh breaking through the tension. "I've told you about calling them that. Just 'cause you haven't set foot in a church since you got caught kissing Bro. Franklin's son in the choir room..."

My mom burst into full laughter.

"I can just imagine your faces when Pastor Booker and Sister Washington turned on the lights!"

"Ha-ha, laugh it up," Brenda replied. "It wasn't funny then. That nosy Sister Washington told everyone in the choir he had his hand up my shirt and my eyes were rolling back. Lies! We were just kissing. One hand was on my butt, the other on my shoulder."

"But why, did Pastor Booker have to base his entire Sunday sermon on it? Lust of the Flesh—really?"

Mom laughed so hard she nearly choked. "Oh yeah, I remember that! The whole choir was trying not to laugh, and there you were in the corner, giving Sister Washington the evil eye and shaking your fist like you wanted to fight."

"She rolled her eyes at me!" Brenda said. "My face was redder than the choir robes."

"You weren't playing," Mom giggled.

"I wasn't! I was ready to fight her. Lying on me like that."

"Sis. Washington was sixty-six!"

"So what? I was still ready to put my foot up her sixty-six-year-old ass," Brenda snapped, and both women burst into uncontrollable laughter.

But then Mom's tone shifted.

"Seriously, though... how's his family taking all of this since you told brother?"

"I talked to his sister—the one who lived down the street from y'all. She said the whole family's turned on him. His mother—sweetest woman you'll ever meet—disowned him. Broke down in tears when she heard what he did to his own kids."

Mom was silent.

"And apparently... this isn't the first time."

"What do you mean?"

"Remember I told you he was married before?"

"Yeah..."

"Well, it turns out he messed with his other daughter too. That's why his ex-wife divorced him."

"I thought you said he caught her cheating?"

"Just one of the many lies he told."

There was a pause. Then Brenda added, "Look, keep your head up. I'm praying for you. Texas is a good move—a fresh start for you and the girls."

"I know," Mom said quietly. "You're right." The girls are going to stay with my sister and her husband till I come down. I have some things I must take care of before I join them.

"I love you, girl. I'll talk to you tomorrow."

"Love you too. Goodnight."

As the click of the receiver echoed softly, I carefully placed the phone back in its cradle, my hands trembling.

"We were hit with surprising news the next morning—we were going to visit our family in Texas for a while."

"Earth to Punkin!" Tiffany said, nudging me with her shoulder.

"Huh?"

"I said I'm hungry. Is there any more ham sandwiches in the bag?"

"Here," I said, handing her the lunch bag Mom packed for the trip. "You can have mine."

"Thanks!" Tiffany said, grabbing the bag like she hadn't eaten in days.

I couldn't believe she was sending us to Texas on our own. Was this some kind of punishment? Or did she just need space — space from us... from me?

Maybe it was because I didn't speak up sooner. Because I stayed silent about what my stepdad was doing.

A tear slid down my cheek as I turned back to the bus window, watching the world blur past.

5

Chapter 5

New Beginnings

"Next stop, Dallas station," the driver announced as I leaned my head against the window and stared out. Skyscrapers towered above the streets, some sharp-edged, others curved in strange, futuristic shapes. And the people—so many people! It was overwhelming.

Back home, we only had two grocery stores: the Mad Butcher and the Piggly Wiggly. Half the roads were dusty, one-lane country streets. Everyone knew everyone. Our idea of fun was a drive-in movie, and the only restaurants that ever stayed busy were Pizza Inn, KFC, and Sonic. Anything else? You had to drive to the next town over.

But here in Dallas, everything was everywhere. Stores on every corner. Restaurants stacked next to each other. The noise, the traffic, the sheer movement of it all—it felt like the city never stopped. I sat back, overwhelmed. How am I supposed to get used to this? I need my quiet time. My books. They've always been my safe place, the one escape from my reality. Is this my new reality now? Everything here moves so fast.

Lord, help me find my place in all of this. Help me fit in. I prayed to myself as I looked out the window at the busy city.

As the bus pulled into the Dallas terminal, I spotted Uncle Joe waiting near the building. A medium build man with light skin and a receding hairline. He was fanning himself with what looked like a piece of cloth, then using it to wipe the sweat from his brow.

Tiffany and I grabbed our bags and made our way off the bus.

"Hey, my beautiful nieces!" Uncle Joe grinned, arms wide open. "Come give your uncle a big ol' hug."

"Hey, Uncle Joe!" we said in unison, wrapping our arms around his waist.

"You girls have gotten so big," he said, hoisting our bags. "Come on, let's get outta this heat before we melt."

As we pulled into the driveway, memories of summers past came flooding back. The garage door slowly rose, and there stood Aunt V, in the doorway, wearing her yellow-and-white polka-dot apron over a brown dress.

She was tall—most of Mom's siblings were over 5'8"—with smooth mocha skin and hair black as coal, always pulled back in a bun. Probably to make it easier to slip on her church hat. Aunt V and Uncle Joe were deeply religious. I remembered the summer we came and had church almost every day— Saturday service, Sunday service, choir rehearsal on Wednesday, Bible study on Thursday...

Wait. Today is Thursday. Bible study!

"There y'all are," Aunt V said as we stepped out of the car. "I've been worried sick. How was the ride?"

"Good," we said at the same time.

"And long," Tiffany added.

"Come here and give me a hug. You've both grown so much!"

We wrapped our arms around her, and as she held us close, she began praying right there in the driveway.

"Heavenly Father, thank You for the safe arrival of my two beautiful nieces. Let them feel Your love and surround them with a hedge of protection, in Jesus' name. Amen."

Then she asked, "You girls hungry?"

"Yes, ma'am," we said, our mouths practically watering as we stepped into the kitchen.

The smell hit us like a warm embrace. Smothered chicken. Collard greens with ham hocks. Baked macaroni and cheese. Sweet potatoes. Hot water cornbread. And not one, but two kinds of cake. Tiffany and I just stood there for a second, stunned by the heavenly aroma.

"Come on now, let's get your things into the room so you can wash up before dinner," Aunt V said.

We shared a look of pure satisfaction, then quickly followed her down the hall.

Once we were cleaned up, we returned to the kitchen, where our younger cousins were already seated at the table.

"You girls remember your cousins from Arkansas?" Aunt V asked.

"Hi," they said in unison, shy smiles on their faces.

We sat down and waited for Uncle Joe to bless the food. Eyes closed, heads bowed.

"Oh Heavenly and gracious Father, we come to You giving thanks for the meal prepared before us, and for the safe arrival of our nieces..."

Then it started.

"THANK YA! Glory, glory, glory, hallelujah!" rang out from the other end of the table.

A swift kick to my ankle pulled me out of the moment. "Ouch," I muttered, cracking one eye open to see Tiffany rolling her eyes. I knew exactly what she was thinking—this prayer is about to go somewhere else. And it did.

Aunt V jumped to her feet, clapping and praising. Uncle Joe followed suit, praying even louder.

I had forgotten how deeply spiritual they were. They praised God for everything. And it went on and on, especially when your stomach was growling and that food was just sitting there in front of you, untouched.

Finally, the prayer ended, and we dug in. The food tasted just as incredible as it smelled.

After dinner, we changed into our church clothes.

It was Thursday night.

Time for Bible study.

6

Chapter 6

Mom's Arrival

Three days had gone by, and finally, the moment we'd been waiting for arrived—our mom was coming. Ding dong. The sound of the doorbell made Stephanie and me freeze, eyes wide with excitement.

"Mommy!" we shouted in unison, peeking through the window to see our familiar old car parked in front of the house.

We bolted to the living room just as the door opened, and there she was—our mom, stepping inside with a tired smile.

"MOMMY!" we cried, rushing toward her and wrapping her in the biggest hug we could manage.

"Hey, my babies," she said, kissing us on the forehead. "I've missed you both so much."

"We missed you too," I whispered, burying my face into her chest, inhaling the comfort I'd been longing for.

"Alright now, let your momma breathe," Aunt V said with a chuckle. "You'll have plenty of time to smother her later. Come rest, Marie."

She led Mom to the couch, and just like that, we knew—it was "grown folks' time." Tiffany and I slipped outside to grab the bags from the car.

But something was off.

The front seat and the backseat were packed. Not just with Mom's things—but ours, too. Tiffany and I exchanged confused glances.

"What does this mean?" she asked me.

"I don't know," I said quietly.

Tiffany's questions came quickly, one after another. "Are we not going back? What about school? My friends? What ab—"

"I said I don't know, Tiff!" I snapped.

She looked hurt, and immediately I regretted my tone.

"Let's just bring everything in. I'm sure Mom will explain later."

As we started unloading the car, I noticed Tiffany wiping her eyes. I dropped the bag I was carrying and wrapped her in a hug.

"I'm sorry for yelling. I'm just scared too. But I know everything's going to be okay."

Her voice cracked as she asked, "Is it my fault? Is all this happening because I said something?"

"Stop that," I said firmly. "It's not your fault. It's not mine either. We did what we had to do. We couldn't keep living like that."

I looked up at the sky as tears welled in my eyes, remembering the pain, the fear, the secrets.

"He can't hurt us anymore," I whispered, holding Tiffany tighter.

We stood there on the sidewalk, arms wrapped around each other. We were trying to be strong—but inside, we were both still shattered.

Weeks passed, and we started to settle in our new lives. School was just days away, and the closer it got, the more my stomach turned into knots.

I was about to start high school in a completely new place, without my friends, cousins—without anyone who knew me. Back home, 9th grade was still middle school. But here, I'd be walking halls with kids who looked grown.

I didn't feel ready.

Tiffany, on the other hand, was buzzing with excitement. She was up early, laying out clothes, chatting nonstop about the first day. I stayed buried in bed, wishing I could disappear.

She was always the outgoing one. The one who lit up a room. People noticed her. They listened to her. She connected with everyone, so easily.

Me? I always felt invisible.

I never knew how to talk to people. I never wanted to, really. Books were my world—my escape. Tiffany was taller than me, too, and most people assumed she was the older one. Her complexion was lighter, a warm caramel, while mine was more of a milk chocolate. I always felt like she got more attention because of it.

So I faded into the background and let her shine.

That's what big sisters do… right?

At least, that's what I told myself. But deep down, I knew the truth—I was just afraid. Afraid to speak. Afraid to be seen. Afraid to upset anyone, to say the wrong thing, to not be liked.

So I smiled. And shut down. And hid behind what everyone wanted me to be.

The first day of my new school was exactly what I feared. The halls were packed with kids who looked older than me, taller, louder, already like they knew who they were. Boys walked by in Adidas and Nike tracksuits, gold chains resting on their chests. Girls wore short shorts and even shorter skirts, big gold hoop earrings, high-top sneakers, moving through the halls like they belonged there.

I felt completely out of place in my long blue jean skirt and white short-sleeved button-down. I tried to make myself smaller as I walked, hoping not to be noticed. When lunchtime came, I sat alone, keeping my head down, avoiding eye contact. It was just me and my books—my shield, my excuse, my way of disappearing.

Eventually, we moved into our own place. Mom got a job at the hospital. We became members of Aunt V's church. Tiffany and I even made a few friends.

From the outside, everything looked good.

But inside, I still felt like I didn't belong. Like love was something just out of reach. Something for other people, not me.

Our neighbors had three kids we hung out with sometimes. The oldest, Jay, was a couple of years younger than me, but we clicked. One day her parents asked if I'd go with her to her end-of-school dance. It was her first one, and they wanted someone to keep an eye on her. I agreed. It made me feel useful, and I figured it would be mostly younger kids anyway.

But I was wrong.

That night wasn't just a dance.

It was the beginning of something I couldn't have imagined. A chapter of my life that would follow me for years.

The night I met him.

7

Chapter 7

The beginning "A Love Story"

We pulled up to Jay's school, and immediately I noticed something strange—the building looked dim, almost eerie. It had no windows, which struck me as unsettling. I couldn't help but wonder: do the students feel trapped inside, like prisoners waiting for the bell to release them so they can finally feel the sun on their skin?

Inside, the dance was surprisingly magical. The decorations were beautiful, creating an atmosphere that felt light and dreamy—nothing like what I expected from such a cold-looking building. This was the first dance I'd been to since we moved, and I had no idea what to wear. I thought the dress code would be dressy casual, but most of the kids were in jeans and sneakers. Meanwhile, I stood out in a light pink silk dress that fell past my knees, ruffles at the bottom, lace across the chest, white stockings, and my shiny off-white church shoes.

I felt completely out of place.

My anxiety crept in quickly, and I found myself backing up to the wall, watching Jay from a distance. She danced with her friends, laughing and glowing with energy. I stayed where I was, quietly swaying to the beat, trying to blend in.

And then he appeared.

"Man, who is that?" Sam asked his boys as they scanned the dance floor. They were checking out every girl who walked by, trying to guess their age, deciding who was old enough to get a number from.

I overheard some chaperons say, Sam and his friends weren't supposed to be there—they went to the high school down the street and had crashed the middle school dance. He started asking around about me, but no one seemed to know who I was. One of his friends nudged him. "Just go talk to her, man."

And so, he did.

As he walked toward me, my heart pounded. My legs felt weak. He had this big, confident smile and mesmerizing brown eyes. When he finally stood in front of me, he asked my name.

"Shauntilia," I said nervously, "but everyone calls me Punkin."

"Punkin, huh? Well, Miss Shauntilia, would you like to dance?"

I nodded, but my body didn't move. My mind raced—What if I don't know how to dance? What if I look ridiculous?

As I started to step back, he gently reached for my hand and led me onto the dance floor. He pulled me close, and suddenly, this warm sensation washed over me. My body trembled.

"I got you," he whispered into my ear. "I won't let you fall."

I looked up into his eyes, then rested my head against his chest, listening to the beat of his heart. It felt like we were the only two people in the room, slow dancing in our own little world. Until the DJ switched it up and blasted Tony! Toni! Toné!'s "It Feels Good." The tempo change broke the spell.

Sam grinned and started dancing around me like nobody was watching, singing loudly, "If it really feels good to you, baby, let me hear you say, uh uh baby!"

I laughed, and we left the dance floor together. We talked for the rest of the night. When he asked for my number, his friends crowded around, curious about the mystery girl who had caught Sam's attention. He tore a napkin from the table and waited for me to recite my number. I did, still in disbelief that this was happening. Then he gave me his number.

His friends were stunned—he had never done that before.

I left the dance with the biggest smile on my face.

"Oooh, I saw you dancing with Sam!" Jay teased, linking arms with me as we walked outside.

"Did you get his number?"

"I did," I said, showing it to her. She beamed, talking about how much fun the night was, but I could barely hear her—I was lost in thoughts of him. His smooth voice, the way he held me, the scent of his cologne still lingering on my dress. His confidence amazed me. Everyone loved him—students, even his old teachers.

It felt like a dream.

But as the night faded, doubt crept in. What if it's all in my head? What if he doesn't really like me? I stood in front of the mirror later that night, staring at my reflection, the familiar insecurities rising up again. I'm not pretty enough. Not smart enough. I'm damaged. Who could really love me?

The next day, I woke up with a tiny spark of hope. Maybe—just maybe—he'd call.

It was lunchtime when the phone rang. My sister darted to answer it. It was almost always for her anyway.

"Hi, can I speak to Shauntilia?" a voice asked.

Her eyes got wide. "Really? Who is this?"

"Sam."

She turned to me, grinning. "It's for you… Saaaam," she said, dragging out his name with a teasing smile.

My heart dropped. I couldn't believe it—he actually called.

I grabbed the phone. "Hello?" I said, my voice shaky.

"Was that your sister?" he asked, chuckling.

"Yeah," I replied.

"Are you surprised I called?"

"A little," I admitted, though in my head I was screaming, YES! I can't believe this is real!

Over the next few weeks, we talked every day. Then one day, he asked if he could stop by.

"Stop by?" I repeated, nervously.

"Sure... I just need to ask my mom."

I did, and she said it was okay.

The moment I hung up, the nerves hit me like a wave. It's one thing to talk on the phone—but face to face? What if he didn't like me once he really saw me? Just a quiet, sheltered girl who found comfort in books and dreams instead of reality.

I panicked trying to find something to wear and settled on a pair of jeans, a tie-dye shirt, and my white Payless sneakers. I loved jeans—probably because we weren't allowed to wear them for so long. It wasn't considered proper in our old church. But once Mom started studying the Bible for herself, everything began to change. She changed.

A lot had changed since that night. And things were never the same.

Then—knock knock.

He was here.

My sister sat on the couch watching TV. Mom was at the dining table, nibbling on the roast she was cooking. My sister moved to answer the door, but I jumped up.

"I got it. Sit down!"

They were just as curious to meet him as I was nervous.

I opened the door—and there he was. Smelling amazing, dressed head to toe in Adidas. Hat, jacket, pants, and shoes all matching.

"Hey, beautiful," he said, leaning in for a hug.

As we embraced, he noticed my mom.

"Heeeey, momma," he said, walking straight over and hugging her like they'd known each other forever.

"I'm Sam. Mmm, what's that smell? It's amazing."

"Roast and potatoes," she said with a smile.

"Oooh, can I get a plate?"

She laughed. "Sure."

My sister and I exchanged stunned looks as he casually walked toward the kitchen like he lived there. I followed him, ready to show him around—but he already had it under control, searching cabinets like he'd done it before.

You know the saying, make yourself at home?

Well, he did. And somehow… I was loving every second of it.

8

Chapter 8

Will You Be Mine

It had been almost a month since Sam and I started talking, though we never officially defined what we were. Sam was popular, a bit of a class clown, and a *natural smooth talker.* Everyone loved him. No matter where we went, someone would shout, "What's up, Sam?" or call out, "Heeey Sam!" with a smile or a playful wave. He thrived in the spotlight, soaking up the attention. Me? I was the opposite. I shrank back, trying to stay unnoticed, especially when his friends came around. I'd quietly fade into the background, content watching from the sidelines.

Today was different. It was the day I'd finally meet his siblings. He had asked my mom earlier that day if it was okay for me to come over, and to my surprise—she said yes.

Normally Sam drove himself, but this time one of his friends dropped him off and he told me we'd be walking to his house. I didn't mind. It just meant more time alone with him, and that was all I needed.

The walk felt endless, but the time we shared made it worth it. We laughed, talked, and every second felt special. Eventually, I began to slow down, my legs starting to ache. He noticed right away.

"You tired?" he asked, stopping in his tracks.

I nodded, a little embarrassed. That's when he turned his back to me and crouched down.

"Hop on—I'll carry you."

At first, I thought he was joking. But then I felt his hand gently touch my leg as he pulled me closer. My heart skipped a beat. I froze, staring at him like a deer caught in headlights.

He glanced back at me, grinning. "I'm serious. Get on."

Slowly, I wrapped my arms around his neck, then my legs around his waist, still unsure this was actually happening. He stood up with ease, like I weighed nothing at all, and carried me the rest of the way—strong, confident, and effortlessly cool.

In that moment, I felt seen. Protected. And a little more like I belonged.
  We finally made it to his house, which was just around the corner from his high school. I met his siblings, and they welcomed me with open, loving arms. His mom, a nurse, wasn't home at the time, and to be honest, I felt a bit relieved. I didn't know what to say to her or how she might treat me.

I was sitting on the couch with one of his sisters, who was holding their little baby brother, when the front door suddenly opened. A short, slim woman with a youthful face walked in. It was his mother. She stood in front of me wearing a crisp white nursing uniform—white stockings, white shoes, and a white nurse's cap perched on top of her big, bouncing brown curls. She was a beautiful woman, and I couldn't help but think, so that's where Sam gets his looks.

She leaned over and took her son from his sister's arms, then asked, "Who is this? You all know you're not supposed to have company over when I'm not here, especially someone I don't know."

"Sam brought her over," his sister replied.

Just then, Sam came walking in from the kitchen with a sandwich in his hand and mustard at the corners of his mouth.

"Hey, Momma," he said, going in for a hug. "This is Shauntilia, my girlfriend."

Girlfriend? He'd never called me that before. I'm his girlfriend? A rush of nerves surged through me. I was stunned, speechless, sitting there with a confused grin on my face. Finally, I managed to say, "Nice to meet you."

His mom responded, "Girlfriend, huh? Nice to meet you too, baby. Y'all go get those groceries out the car," and then disappeared into her room.

I was so nervous, I leaned over to Sam and told him I wanted to go home.

"Are you scared of my mom?" he asked.

Terrified—but I said no.

"Stay for dinner," he said. "Then we'll go."

"...Okay."

Lord, help me not be scared, I prayed silently, feeling out of place as I looked around at all the beautiful things in their home. But as the evening went on, his mom warmed up to me. We had a lovely dinner, and by the time I offered to help clear the table, she looked at me with a smile—one that felt like she was giving me her approval.

Later, she let Sam drive me home. I floated the entire way, completely on cloud nine. A Mint Condition song came on the radio—Pretty Brown Eyes— and it made me smile. I turned my head, sneaking a glance at Sam, trying to catch his hazel-brown eyes. He noticed and met my gaze. I blushed.

He smiled, reached for my hand, and laced his fingers through mine. I tried to hide the rush of emotions flooding through me, but for the first time in a long while, I felt truly happy.

A year has passed despite the weight of my insecurities and the scars of my past, I finally let myself surrender. Through steadfast love and boundless patience, Sam taught me that I am not only worthy of love but also capable of embracing it.

I've noticed my mom's spirit changing every day. We used to be in church all the time, but now she works constantly, and we rarely go. Throughout the school years, she made sure we had everything we needed. Still, I worry about her. I think the weight of everything that happened to us—the secrets that were kept—was slowly wearing her down.

Time moved on, as it always does. The girl who once sat nervously in her boyfriend's living room—the same girl who gave her virginity to someone who made her feel seen, special, and loved, even when the idea of being touched once terrified her—began to fade. She carried the weight of feeling like damaged goods, believing that only God could ever truly love her. But over time, she slowly became a young woman, shaped by love, hard lessons, and life's quiet storms. I didn't know it then, but that chapter was just the beginning of a much bigger story.

It's my senior year — where are you Sam? As I look around, I see couples wrapped in each other's arms, while I'm sitting here alone, waiting for the school bus to take me home. You used to be the one picking me up, smiling like nothing could ever go wrong. You said your mom was sending you to California for a few days. But days turned into weeks, and weeks into months. My heart aches for you. No calls, no letters — it's like you vanished. I keep replaying the past couple of years in my head, wondering if it was something I did, or didn't do to make you not want to see me anymore. I just don't understand.

9

Chapter 9

Was It Real?

Behind our apartments was the Red Bird Recreation Center, where my sister, a few friends, and I would often go to watch the guys play basketball. One day, I was sitting in the bleachers, lost in one of my romantic novels and daydreaming about Sam, when I heard a voice call out from the bottom of the stands, "Hey, why are you sitting up there by yourself?" I peeked over my book and saw a group of cute guys standing on the court. I figured they couldn't possibly be talking to me, so I went back to my reading. But then, I felt the bleachers shake as someone ran up toward me. Before I knew it, my book was gently snatched from my hands. "Did you not hear me talking to you?" he said. I looked up — and there he was, this high-yellow guy with light brown, dreamy eyes. He was gorgeous!

I just sat there, staring into his eyes, completely shocked. I couldn't believe it — it was Lonnie, one of the most popular guys in the neighborhood. He had a bit of a bad boy reputation, and everyone seemed to show him respect — maybe even fear him a little.

"Oh, I didn't know you were talking to me," I finally said.

He sat down beside me, still holding my book hostage, glancing at the title — He's Always Been Mine — and reading it out loud with a little smirk before flipping it over to check out the back cover.

"So this is a love story, huh?" he asked.

I lowered my eyes shyly. "Yes. Can I have my book back, please?"

He chuckled. "Please? Ain't you proper," he teased. Then he added, "They call you Punkin, right?"

"Yes," I mumbled, barely looking up.

"Let me get your number," he said casually.

I looked up at him, surprised. "My number?"

"Yeah, so I can call you sometime," he said, smiling.

I couldn't believe it. Was he serious? Everyone kept telling me I should move on, but with him? A million thoughts raced through my mind.

Still, I found myself scribbling my number down and handing it to him.

"Cool," Lonnie said, handing my book back. "Imma call you."

He stood up and jogged back down the bleachers to rejoin his friends.

I sat there in a daze, wondering, Why me? What could he possibly see in plain, ordinary me?

A couple of days passed with no word from Lonnie. I couldn't understand why I was thinking about him so much — we had only shared that one brief encounter. But those eyes, and the way he looked at me, kept replaying in my mind.

Stop it, Punkin, I told myself. There's no way he's going to call. It must have been a joke — probably just him and his friends messing around. He could have any girl he wanted.

And there I was again, drowning in my insecurities.

I sat by the window, staring out at the little wall outside our apartment where everyone liked to hang out. I noticed my sister sitting there with her boyfriend when a car pulled up. She walked over, talked to someone inside, then turned and pointed right at me, sitting in the window.

A group of guys climbed out of the car — and then I saw the driver.

Lonnie.

My heart nearly stopped. Was he coming over here?

I jumped off the couch, realizing there was no way to hide — he had definitely seen me. I sprinted down the hallway, panicking. My hair's a mess, I look horrendous! I thought as I tore through my closet, trying to find something to wear.

I was frantically pulling my hair into a ponytail when a knock sounded at the door. I froze, forcing myself to breathe and pull myself together. With every step toward the door, I moved slowly, trying to steady my breath.

Even though I was terrified, I opened the door.

"Hey, hey," I said, stuttering as I struggled to get the words out. "What are you doing here?"

"I came to see what you were up to and ask why I haven't seen you at the rec," Lonnie said, flashing that smile that had won me over in the first place. "I kinda missed you."

W-what? I couldn't believe what I was hearing. He missed me? That couldn't be true... could it? I thought to myself.

"You're just messing with me," I said.

"No, for real. Come outside. Why are you cooped up in the house anyway?"

He really don't know me. I hardly ever go outside and hang out. My sister has always been the outgoing one — she makes friends easily and loves being the center of attention. Me, on the other hand, I shy away from all that. Give me a good book and I'm happy.

"I just started a new book," I told him.

"You already finished the other one? Dang, that book was thick!" he said, sounding impressed.

"Yeah, and now I'm on the second in the series," I replied.

Lonnie grabbed my book again and grinned.

"No way — I gotta get you out of the house," he said, then took my hand and led me outside.

Everyone outside—those sitting on the wall and lounging in their parked cars—stared at us as we walked past. We crossed the street to the park and sat on the bleachers facing the soccer field.

"Tell me about yourself," he said, pulling a bag of M&M's from his pocket.

I stared at the yellow bag as my stomach growled loudly. Embarrassed, I clutched my stomach.

"Wow," he laughed, offering me the candy.

I smiled and held out my hand. "Thanks," I said as he poured them into my palm.

"What a way to break the ice," he said.

We both laughed and began talking about our lives. I wanted to ask him why he had stopped attending school and what had led him to sell drugs, but I knew that would have been a little too much—for now.

Lonnie and I had been dating for a few weeks now, and I couldn't stop thinking about that bad boy side of him as I stared out the window of his car. There was something about the way he demanded respect — and got it — that intrigued me. I'd seen him get tough with people when it came to his hustle, but never with me. Everyone called him "Lil Wimp," but there was nothing wimpy about him. To me, he was just Lonnie.

We were on our way to his house so I could meet his family for the first time. I was a little nervous — not just about the whole meet-the-family thing, but because Lonnie lived on the other side of town. The side people called the "real hood" part of Oak Cliff.

As we drove through the neighborhood, Lonnie must've picked up on the tension in my body and the worry in my eyes.

"Don't be scared. I run this side. You don't have anything to worry about," he said, trying to calm my nerves.

But honestly, it didn't help much.

We turned down Alabama Street, where he lived. I found myself trying to remember every detail — street names, the colors of buildings, store signs — just in case I needed to tell someone where to come find me. I knew I had to shake the fear, but it wasn't easy.

When we pulled up in front of his house, I saw his mom sitting on the porch with a couple of her friends. They were drinking beers and gossiping about whatever was going on in the neighborhood. She was in a chair that looked just a little too small for her, holding a cigarette between her fingers.

We got out of the car, and she stared us down — mostly me. My heart pounded in my chest. I was beyond nervous.

"Whose car you driving '? You better not be parking a hot car in front of my house," she said.

Hot car? Was I riding around in a stolen car? My anxiety went into overdrive.

He glanced at his mom, clearly caught off guard, and gave her a quick side-eye as we walked up to the porch where she and her friends were sitting.

"Well, who's this pretty little thing you brought with you?" she asked.

"This my girl, Punkin," he said.

She gave me a long stare, like she was sizing me up. I smiled nervously and said, "Nice to meet you," then greeted everyone else on the porch.

"Oh, you got yourself a nice, polite one," she said with a little giggle, glancing at her friends.

I managed a smile, but inside, I was shaking. I've never liked being the center of attention — all those eyes on me always make me feel uncomfortable.

We went inside so I could meet his siblings. His little brothers were sprawled on the couch, watching cartoons.

"Hey, y'all," he said. "This is my girl, Punkin."

They lifted their heads at the same time, glanced at me, said hey, and then went right back to the TV.

His sister stepped out from a back room and paused in the doorway. "Hi, I'm

Trice," she said.

"Nice to meet you," I replied, nodding.

"Do you know how to braid?" she asked.

"Yeah."

"Okay, good." She grabbed my hand before I could say anything else. I glanced back at Lonnie as she pulled me toward her room. He just shrugged and smiled.

"Can you put my hair in two braids?" she asked. "My mom can't really part it straight."

"Sure," I said, as she handed me a small comb.

I started on her hair, and she talked nonstop the entire time. Lonnie leaned in the doorway, watching us with a smile.

"You want something to drink?" he asked.

"No, I'm fine."

I order a pizza it will be here soon. He said as he walked in the room at sat on his sister's bed beside me. He stayed with me as I finished her hair.

After we finished eating, we said our goodbyes and headed towards the door. As kind as his family was, I felt a small sense of relief that we hadn't stayed too long. I was ready to return to where I felt most at ease—alone with him

While we rode in the car, he held my hand, occasionally glancing over at me with a warm smile that made my heart flutter.

Could this really be love I'm feeling again?

10

Chapter 10

You

I couldn't stop thinking about Lonnie — it was like I needed to be near him constantly. But deep down, a part of me still carried the weight of what I'd felt for Sam. I really loved Sam. He was my first real love, the kind that stays with you, even after it ends. There was something so natural and easy about the way we connected, like he just understood me without me having to explain.

But with Lonnie, everything felt more intense — like fire compared to warmth. When he asked me to come over, I always said yes, even if it meant skipping school. I think I was scared — scared that if I didn't, he'd stop loving me and disappear, just like Sam did.

I had just left Lonnie's and was riding the bus home, thinking about the time we'd spent together and what might happen if I didn't make it back before my mom did. As I stepped off the bus, I kept hearing a car horn honking repeatedly.

Once the bus finally pulled away, I heard a familiar voice calling my name from across the street.

"Shauntilia!"

I froze. That voice… it couldn't be.

Sam?!

I shouted his name in disbelief as I saw him stepping out of a car and crossing the street toward me. My heart swelled with emotion — joy and hurt crashing into each other all at once.

As he got closer, I didn't know what to do — hug him, kiss him… or hit him for leaving me the way he did.

"Shauntilia, it's been a minute. How have you been?" he asked.

"Fine," I replied, eyeing him from head to toe, trying to hold myself together. I turned and started walking toward home, but he reached out and grabbed my arm.

"Wait — I want to talk to you." I gently placed my hand on his wrist and slid free from his grip.

"Then keep up, because I've got somewhere to be," I said, picking up my pace, making him work if he really wanted this conversation. "What do you want, Sam?" I asked without looking back. "I can tell you're mad. Just slow down so I can talk to you," he said.

He caught up to me and grabbed my arm again, stepping in front of me and forcing me to stop. "For real — let's talk," he said, his voice more serious now. "I'm listening. Go ahead."

He didn't speak right away. He just looked into my eyes, and I could see the pain written all over his face. It hit me like a wave — sorrow, regret… something real. I saw the tears beginning to form before he even said a word.

Then he told me everything — why he had to leave, the trouble he got himself into, how his mom ended up sending him to California. And as much as it hurt to relive the way he left me — the silence, the lies — one thing still remained true. I still loved him.

We sat outside my house, just catching up. It felt like old times — easy, familiar, like no time had passed at all.

"You gonna invite me in?" he asked, smiling.

"Sure, come on," I said, but a voice in my head screamed, What are you doing? I had a man now. Sam left me heartbroken, alone, and confused… and yet, here I was, letting him into my space like none of that ever happened.

Inside, I motioned toward the couch. "Make yourself comfortable. Want something to drink?"

"You know I remember where everything is. I'll grab something in a minute," he replied casually.

"Okay, I'm gonna see who's home." I started down the hallway. "Mom? You here?" I called out. Silence. I peeked into her room. Empty. Tiffany's room too.

That's weird, I thought.

As I turned to head back, I nearly jumped out of my skin — Sam was suddenly right in front of me, holding a piece of paper.

"Boy, you scared me! What's that?" "I saw it on the fridge when I went to grab a drink," he said, handing it to me.

It was a note from my mom — she was working a double shift. Stephanie was staying over at a friend's.

Perfect, I thought sarcastically. The only reason I let him in was because I figured I wouldn't be alone.

"So... we're all alone," he said, giving me a look I remembered all too well. "Don't get any ideas," I said quickly. "You lost those privileges a long time ago."

We both laughed lightly, walking back toward the living room. But he stopped suddenly in front of my bedroom door, eyes locked on something.

His expression changed.

He was staring at a photo taped to my mirror — a picture of Lonnie and me. I'd taken down most of the old memories, but this one... this one was new. It wasn't of us. It was of me and someone else. The hurt in his eyes was impossible to ignore. He didn't even have to speak — his face said everything.

But then he turned to me and asked quietly, "Do you love him?"

His question hit me harder than I expected. Do you love him?

I opened my mouth to answer, but nothing came out. My eyes dropped to the picture on the mirror — Lonnie's arm around me, both of us smiling like we didn't have a care in the world. And for a while, we didn't.

I looked back at Sam. His eyes were searching mine, waiting. Hoping.

"I..." I paused, suddenly aware of the storm brewing in my chest. "Lonnie's been good to me. He's been there when I needed someone. He makes me feel safe."

Sam looked down, nodding slowly, as if bracing for what was coming.

"But you..." I continued, my voice softening, "you were my first real love. That doesn't just disappear. I tried to hate you for leaving, for not explaining, for letting me hurt like that... but I couldn't. I still think about you, and sometimes, I still feel everything."

He looked up, eyes glassy with emotion.

"I don't know what that means," I admitted. "I'm with Lonnie now, and I care about him. But I'd be lying if I said I didn't still love you."

Silence hung between us like thick air. Then Sam spoke, his voice low. "That's all I needed to hear."

Silence lingered in the air, heavy and full of everything we hadn't said over the past months.

Sam stepped closer, his eyes never leaving mine. "I don't want to mess things up for you," he said. "But I had to know... if there was still something here. Because I never stopped loving you."

I felt my breath catch. Every part of me was screaming for clarity, but none of it made sense — not with him this close. Not with his voice sounding like home and heartbreak all at once.

He raised his hand slowly, brushing a curl away from my face like he used to. His fingers lingered just a second too long.

"I shouldn't," I whispered, though I wasn't even sure who I was trying to convince — him or myself.

But then he leaned in. And I didn't stop him. Our lips met — soft at first, uncertain, then full of all the words we hadn't said. The kiss tasted like memories, like pain and longing, like love that had never really left.

When we finally pulled apart, I stepped back, heart pounding.

"That shouldn't have happened," I said, eyes searching his. "But it did," he replied, his voice quiet but certain.

11

Chapter 11

Guilty Pleasures

The next morning, I sat at the kitchen table, lost in thought. My coffee had gone cold, the spoon still slowly circling inside the cup. I couldn't stop replaying last night — the way Sam held me, how his hands moved gently over my skin, and how he whispered "I love you" like he meant it with every breath.

His kiss lingered on my neck like a secret I didn't know how to carry. "Punkin!"

My mom's voice snapped me back to reality.

"Yes, ma'am?" "Telephone," she said, handing me the cordless phone. I took it, heart already pounding. "Hello?"

"Hey — what happened to you last night?" Lonnie's voice came through. "I called a bunch of times and you didn't pick up."

Oh God. Lonnie.

Panic twisted in my stomach. What was I supposed to say? "I let it ring, but the machine came on," he added. "You know I hate leaving messages on that thing." "Yeah," I said, forcing my voice to stay steady. "The ringer must've been off." But my hand was shaking. And I could already feel the weight of the lie pressing down on my chest.

"I've got a special surprise for you this weekend," he said.

"Oh really?" I replied, a hint of excitement slipping into my voice. "What is it?"

"You'll just have to wait and see. You coming over today?"

I hesitated. I wanted to say yes. I wanted to see him — to pretend everything was normal. But the guilt was heavy, and the shame even heavier. I couldn't face him. Not yet.

"Not today," I said quietly. "But I'll come by in the morning before my interview at Grandy's."

"Alright," he said. "I'll call you later. Make sure that ringer's on this time."

We both laughed, the sound light but my heart anything but, before I hung up the phone.

How am I supposed to keep this secret? It feels so heavy inside me, pressing down on my chest. I only have one person I could possibly talk to about this. I walked to my room, collapsed onto my bed, and stared up at the ceiling. Can I really trust her with something like this? What should I do?

At some point, I must have dozed off, because when I opened my eyes, it was past three. Oh no—lunch with Mekia! She's going to be furious. This is the third time I've stood her up. Where's my phone? I need to call her.

Mekia was one of my closest friends. We met at the beginning of my sophomore year. She came from a big family with even bigger personalities. Outspoken and fearless, Mekia didn't take mess from anyone.

As I walked into the living room, I noticed the red light blinking on the answering machine. A message. My heart jumped. I hoped it was Sam, but part of me feared it might be Lonnie. I pressed the button, my finger trembling with both dread and hope.

"Hey, I'm going to have to cancel our late lunch. How about an early dinner? Hit me back."

A wave of relief washed over me. I didn't want to disappoint her again. Grabbing the cordless phone, I started dialing as I made my way to the kitchen for a granola bar.

"Hello?"

"Hey, Mekia," I said, trying to sound upbeat. I had missed talking to her.

"Hey, Punkin. So, are we still on for dinner, or are you calling to cancel again because of Lonnie?" I laughed lightly, trying to mask the guilt. "No, no. Just calling to say I'm in."

The truth was, I felt awful. I'd been a terrible friend lately—putting Lonnie before her, just like I did back when I was with Sam.

"Okay, I'll come pick you up around six," she said, clearly excited. "I got my brother's car." "Perfect. See you at six. Bye, girl."

As I hung up, my mind began to spin. There was so much I wanted—no, needed—to tell her. But could I trust her with this betrayal?

I turned on the radio as I got ready to meet Mekia for dinner, singing along to every song that came on. While doing my hair, a familiar tune started playing—If I Ever Fall in Love by Shai.

"And if I ever, ever fall in love again, I will be sure that the lady is a friend..." My heart dropped.

Oh my God— I begin to think about last night...that's the song. The one that played last night as we lay there, tangled in silence after making love. I remember Sam breaking down in tears, holding me so tightly, knowing it would be the last time. The last time he'd ever hold me like that.

Tears welled up and began streaming down my face as the memory took over. I could still see the heartbreak in his eyes as he slowly unwrapped his arms from around me, sat up, and quietly began getting dressed. That look— I'll never forget it. It pierced straight through me, deeper than I thought anything could.

Beep, beep!

A car horn snapped me out of the moment. I glanced out the window—there was Mekia, looking up at me with a wide smile. She rolled down the window and waved, yelling, "Come on, girl!" as she belted out Ain't 2 Proud 2 Beg by TLC—loudly and completely off-key.

I couldn't help but laugh as I waved back. Turning from the window, I quickly wiped my face and tried to fix the mess my mascara had made.

As I made my way down the stairs, I saw Mekia outside the car, dancing like nobody was watching—just being her usual, ridiculous, lovable self. I smiled to myself.

I really love that girl. She always knows how to lift my spirits, even when she doesn't know I need it. She's a true friend—one I honestly believe God placed in my life for a time like this.

As I stepped off the last stair, I danced my way over to Mekia with a big grin.

"I've missed your crazy butt!" I laughed as we hugged like we hadn't seen each other in years.

"I've missed you too, girlie!" she said, squeezing me tight.

We climbed into the car, blasting the music and singing at the top of our lungs. It felt just like old times—free, light, and full of laughter.

At the restaurant, we talked and laughed about everything under the sun—except the one thing that had my mind spinning.

After dinner, we moved to the patio, where we sat under the stars. I stared up at the sky, my thoughts weighing me down.

"But for real—how are you?" she asked gently, reaching over to grab my hand. Her eyes searched mine as I tried to mask the heaviness in my heart, but I knew she could see through me.

"I'm..." I paused. I wanted to say I'm good, but the words wouldn't come. I needed to get this secret off my chest. I needed her advice. But what would she think of me once she knew?

My heart started to race, and tears welled up, falling down my cheeks before I could stop them.

"What is it? What's going on?" she asked, her voice filled with concern.

I stared down at the tear stains forming on the hem of my shirt. "I... I cheated on Lonnie with Sam," I mumbled.

The words barely left my lips before a lump formed in my throat and my stomach turned. I couldn't look at her. I just stared at the ground, ashamed and afraid of what I'd see in her eyes.

But she gently squeezed my hand. "It's going to be okay. Sam was the love of your life. That kind of love doesn't just disappear."

I looked up at her, stunned. "You must think I'm a terrible person."

"No! You have a good heart—you're a good person. I could never think that about you," she said firmly. "Everyone goes through something like this. I did, too."

"What?" I asked, surprised. "You went through something like this?"

She nodded. "Remember Joshua? The guy who broke my heart last year?"

"Of course. You were madly in love with him—then he cheated on you with Tiffany."

"Yeah, well... four months ago, I was out on a date with Tony—you know, the guy I got with after Joshua—and out of nowhere, Joshua paged me. I called him back, and he started apologizing again, saying he missed me, wanted to see me. So, I went to his place... and one thing led to another and... bam."

She held out her hand. A sparkling ring caught the light.

"We're engaged."

My eyes widened. "Whoa! It's beautiful!" I grabbed her hand for a closer look. "Why didn't you tell me?"

"I don't know. You've been so wrapped up with Lonnie lately, and we haven't had time to really talk." "I'm happy for you," I said, pulling her into a hug.

And I was. I was truly happy for her. But the guilt of what I had done still clung to me. No matter how much I smiled, it didn't erase the betrayal I carried inside.

We spent the rest of the night talking about her engagement and everything that lay ahead. It was a welcome distraction; for a little while it took my mind off what I was going through.

"Will you be my maid of honor?" she asked, the biggest smile on her face.

"Yes—of course I will! You're my best friend. A thousand times, yes." I said it with excitement, then reached across to pull her into the tightest hug, shaking with laughter. "I love you, girl."

"I love you too. Now let's get out of here before they throw us out for being so loud." We both laughed as we gathered our things and headed for the door.

"Thank you for tonight," I said as she parked outside my place.

"No problem—you my girl. I always got your back. You're going to be all right."

As I climbed out of the car I stopped, turned, and hugged her neck. "Thanks for listening. And for not judging." She tapped my forehead playfully. "Girl, you know I love you." We laughed again.

I started up the stairs and froze when I saw someone standing in the breezeway. As I drew closer my jaw dropped and my heart pounded so hard it felt like it might burst. "Lonnie!!"

12

Chapter 12

Uncompromising Love

"Lonnie!" I blurted nervously. "You scared me." For a moment, I panicked — what if he'd overheard my conversation with Mekia? "I didn't know you were coming by. I thought I'd see you tomorrow."

"I just wanted to lay eyes on you," he said, his words slightly slurred. "Since I couldn't reach you the other night... just making sure you're really okay."

Something was off. His posture was unsteady, his light-brown eyes half-closed and bloodshot.

"I'm good," I said quickly, reaching to steady him as he swayed toward me. "How long have you been waiting out here?"

"Not too long. I was around the corner dropping something off, so I decided to stop by. I called earlier—your mom said you were out, but she didn't say with who. Was that Mekia who dropped you off?"

"Yes, that was her." "Oh, that's who you were with, huh?"

"Yes. Who did you think I was with?" He let out a sigh, relief softening his face. "I don't know... I wasn't sure."

Wasn't sure? What did that mean? Did he know something? Thoughts crowded my mind. Get it together, Punkin. "Lonnie... are you drunk?" "Girl, ain't nobody drunk. Let's go in the house."

"No, sir. Not with my mom in there—you must've lost your mind. You're drunk, and I don't want her to see you like this." He smirked. "We're still on for tomorrow, right? I told you I had a special surprise." "Yeah. We're still on." "I'll pick you up around seven." His grin widened. "Okay. I'll be ready."

He leaned in to kiss me, nearly tipping over. When his lips touched mine, guilt swept over me like a wave. What am I doing? Not too long ago I was kissing Sam. Tears threatened, but I forced them back until Lonnie disappeared into the night. Only then did I let myself crumble, waving goodbye with a heavy heart.

As I was walking into the house, the phone rang. "Hello?" "Hey... what you doing?" "Sam?"

"Yeah, it's me." "Why are you calling so late?" "I just wanted to hear your voice. I miss you."

Why did he have to say that? In an instant, all the emotions from the night we spent together came rushing back. "Sam, please don't do that." "Do what?" "You know I love you." "Sam, it's late. And you know I'm seeing someone." "Okay... I'll leave you alone. But I really do still love you."

"Goodnight, Sam." "Goodnight."

I set the phone down, my heart heavy. Why is this happening to me? I thought as I went to run myself a long, much-needed, relaxing bath.

The next morning, I woke up to a vase of beautiful flowers with a note tucked inside: "Beautiful flowers for a beautiful lady." My first thought was, Aww, my man got me flowers.

But then I saw the signature. Xoxo, your first love. Why is he trying to drive me crazy? I thought, carrying the bouquet into the living room to set it on the coffee table. My mom and sister looked at me with knowing smiles. "Which one of you thought it'd be funny to put these by my bed so they were the first thing I saw when I woke up?" I asked. "That would be me," my sister said, raising her hand and laughing. "First love, huh?" my mom chimed in. "Yeah, I heard Sam's back in town," my sister added with a playful grin. "Get out of my business, please," I said, tossing a couch pillow at her, unable to hide my own smile.

"What time is your interview today?" my mom asked as I fixed myself some breakfast.

"It's at three, and I was wondering..." I said, moving closer to her. I grabbed her arm and laid my head on her shoulder. "Could you drop me off on your way to work?" I looked up at her and batted my eyes like a child begging for mercy.

She sighed, but a smile tugged at her lips. "Okay, but you better be ready to walk out that door when I leave."

"Yes, ma'am! I will be," I said, dancing with excitement as I bounced back to the counter to finish eating my breakfast.

Time went by fast. I sat in the interview, smiling and acting professional, but my mind wasn't really there. All I could think about was Lonnie — and the betrayal that was eating away at me.

"You're hired!" The words snapped me back to reality. It was the manager, smiling from behind her desk.

"Oh—thank you," I said, standing to shake her hand. She offered me a free drink as I headed out the door.

At the soda fountain, I stared at the options, trying to decide what to get. That's when I noticed a tan car parked on the side of the building. It looked familiar. Then it hit me — it was Lonnie's friend Randy.

As I stepped outside, Lonnie got out of the passenger seat and started walking toward me.

"How did it go?" he asked.

I walked toward him, almost in slow motion. "It went great," I said, forcing excitement into my voice. "I got the position! I start Monday after fourth period, and I'll be doing the morning rush on weekends."

"That's great," he said, opening the car door for me.

As I slid in, Randy turned around from the driver's seat. "What's up?" he said with a nod.

"Hey," I replied, fastening my seatbelt — checking it twice to make sure it was secure. The last time I'd been in this car, we'd been bouncing all over the place because of the hydraulics Randy had installed.

The closer we got to my house, the faster my heart pounded. Lonnie had told me he had a surprise for me — something that felt both exciting and dreadful. Dreadful because I was holding onto a dark secret I was terrified might slip out. If it did, our relationship would be over.

Randy pulled up in front of my apartment. Lonnie opened the door for me, and I slid out. He took my hand, kissed me, and said, "I'll see you in a couple of hours. Pack a bag."

"What? Pack a bag? What do you have planned, Mr.?"

He smiled. "Don't worry about it. Just be ready."

He kissed me again before I headed up the stairs, my mind spinning as I tried to figure out what was coming next.

I packed my bag and pushed it aside, then lay on my bed, staring at the ceiling, lost in thought.

Should I tell Lonnie what happened here — in this very spot — with Sam?

Or should I just keep it buried inside?

The guilt was eating at me.

Lord, I don't know what to do.

I wanted to talk to my mom about what was going on and see if she had any advice for me. But truthfully, we hadn't been talking much—we were just going through the motions. Over the past few years, I'd noticed her struggling with her faith. She started spending more time with my aunt, who loved the club scene, and now she in a new relationship with a man who thinks the world of her.

She had raised us, sacrificed for us, and deserved every bit of happiness life could give her. I just couldn't help but wonder—at what cost?

Just then, a knock sounded at the door.

I already knew who it was.

It was time to go.

I grabbed my bag and opened the door. Lonnie stood there, smiling, holding a bouquet of flowers — ones that looked almost identical to the ones Sam had given me earlier.

"Oh, thank you," I said, forcing the biggest smile I could as I wrapped him in a hug and kissed him.

"You ready to go?" he asked, his voice full of enthusiasm.

"Yes," I replied, picking up my bag.

He reached out and took it from me.

"Thank you," I said softly as we headed out the door.

The sun was already beginning to set.

We had dinner at Olive Garden, then caught a movie at the drive-in. The night was perfect. I lay against his chest, our hands intertwined, watching the flickering screen under the stars.

As the movie ended, Lonnie turned to me with a grin. "I've got one more surprise."

On the drive back to our side of town, I stared out the window. The city lights blurred against the dark sky, hiding most of the stars, but somehow it still felt peaceful.

Then we pulled into the parking lot of a small hotel not far from my house.
And just like that, the calm vanished. My mind went into overdrive.

"Wait right here," Lonnie said, dashing up the stairs with a look of excitement, like a kid with a new toy. I watched him disappear into one of the rooms, my heart racing. Moments later, he came back down.

"You ready?" he asked, grinning.

I smiled. "Yes."
But inside, I wanted to say not really.

He led me upstairs and stopped in front of a door.
"Hold on," he said, pulling out a blindfold.
I laughed nervously as he tied it around my eyes.

I stood there, filled with anticipation and unease. Then the door creaked open. I heard him move around, then felt his hands on the blindfold, slowly lifting it away.

As my eyes adjusted, I gasped.
The room was glowing with candlelight. Pink and red roses — my favorite — filled every corner. Rose petals covered the floor, the bed, even the table, where a bottle of champagne waited.

I walked over and picked up the bottle, turning toward Lonnie with a half smile.

"I know you don't drink," he said, taking it gently from my hand and setting it down. "But it's our anniversary, and I just want you to have one drink with

66

me."

Looking around at everything he'd done, all the effort he'd put into making the night special, I finally nodded. "Okay. One drink."

He poured us each a glass. I took a sip — and instantly regretted it. The taste was awful.

He laughed at the face I made. "Hold on, I've got something better."

He went to the mini-fridge and pulled out another bottle.
   "Here, try this," he said, pouring out the champagne and replacing it with a dark red drink.

"Wild Irish Rose?" I asked, squinting at the label.

"Yeah," he said with a grin. "I think you'll like this one better."

I took a sip — it wasn't bad.
   He raised his glass for a toast, declaring his love and commitment to me.

Commitment.
   That word cut through me like glass — a painful reminder of what I'd done.

I tipped the glass back and drank until there wasn't a single drop left.

"Whoa," Lonnie said, laughing. "Be careful, that stuff's no joke."

But I was already reaching for the bottle, pouring more into my glass and drinking it like water.

He reached for the cup as I swallowed the last drop. "Okay, slow down. That's enough."

The room started to spin. I grabbed the table to steady myself, looking up into Lonnie's beautiful light brown eyes.

"I love you," I whispered, my voice trembling. "I love you so much it hurts."

A tear rolled down my cheek. Lonnie stepped closer, wiping it away.

"I love you too," he said softly, his lips finding mine.

We lay in bed, our bodies tangled, the air still heavy with heat and silence. The only sound was our breathing — uneven, tangled like our thoughts.

The room was dim, lit only by the flicker of candles that had burned too low. Their shadows danced across the walls, moving with every rise and fall of our chests. His hand found mine, fingers tracing lazy circles against my skin, but my mind was somewhere else — caught between the warmth beside me and the guilt that wouldn't let go.

Every heartbeat felt louder than the last. I could still feel the echo of his touch, the weight of what we'd shared. It should've felt perfect. It should've felt right. But beneath the calm, my heart was pounding for another reason entirely.

He whispered my name — soft, almost unsure — and I turned to face him. His eyes were full of something real, something I didn't deserve. I forced a smile, hoping he couldn't see the storm behind it.

He brushed my hair back, pressed a kiss to my forehead, and for a moment, I let myself believe in the peace of it all. But deep down, I knew — love like this couldn't cover the truth forever. I let myself finally drift off to sleep.

The moonlight crept through the curtains, pale and cold. I woke to the sound of rain tapping against the window — soft, steady, almost like a warning. Lonnie was still asleep beside me, his arm draped loosely across my waist. For a moment, I just stared at him. He looked peaceful, unaware, and it made the guilt in my chest twist even tighter.

I slipped out of bed quietly, wrapping myself in the sheet as I sat at the edge. My head felt heavy, like I hadn't slept at all. Every thought that I'd tried to bury the night before came rushing back, louder than ever.

I couldn't keep it in any longer.

By the time Lonnie stirred awake, I was sitting in the chair by the window, watching the rain slide down the glass. He smiled sleepily, stretching. "You okay, beautiful," he said, voice rough with sleep.

"Yeah," I murmured, not turning around right away.

He sat up, sensing something in my tone. "What's wrong?"

I drew in a shaky breath. My heart pounded so hard it felt like it would crack my ribs. "There's something I need to tell you," I said quietly.

The room fell still. The rain filled the silence between us.

Lonnie frowned, his expression softening with concern. "You're scaring me. What is it?"

I turned toward him then, my hands trembling in my lap. "It's about that night... before the interview, when you called an couldn't get in touch with me," I began, my voice barely above a whisper. "Something happened. Something I didn't mean for to happen."

His eyes searched mine — confusion, then realization, then something darker. The silence that followed was unbearable.

I tried to keep speaking, to explain, but the words caught in my throat. "I didn't plan it. I swear I didn't. It just—"

He cut me off, his voice low. "Who?"

The single word felt like a punch.

My eyes dropped to the floor. "Sam."

Lonnie went still. His jaw tightened, his hand gripping the sheet. He looked away for a long time, breathing through clenched teeth. When he finally spoke, his voice was calm — too calm.

"I just need to know why."

Tears blurred my vision. "I don't know," I whispered. "I was hurt, and angry, and I made a mistake. I've hated myself for it ever since."

He stood up, pacing across the room. The sound of the rain grew louder, filling every pause between his footsteps.

Lonnie didn't say a word at first. The silence in the room felt sharp enough to cut through.
   He stood there, staring at me, eyes full of disbelief that slowly turned into anger.

"I trusted you," he finally said, voice trembling. "Everything we've been through... and this is what you do?"

"Lonnie, please—"

He stepped back, shaking his head. "Don't. Just don't."

He ran a hand over his face, pacing once, twice, before stopping at the door. For a second, I thought he was leaving again. But then he turned back to me.

"I can't even look at you right now," he said quietly. "You need to go."

"What?"

"You heard me." His voice cracked but didn't soften. "Just... go."

I grabbed my things from the chair, fumbling as I tried to hold myself together. The air felt cold now — sharp, heavy.

"Lonnie—"

He didn't answer. He just opened the door and stared past me, refusing to meet my eyes.

So I stepped out, my heart pounding, the sound of rain still echoing down the hallway. The door shut behind me with a quiet, final click.

I stood there for a long time, listening, waiting — hoping he might open it again. But he didn't.

And that's when I realized this wasn't just the end of a night.
    It was the beginning of everything falling apart.
    I sat on the stairs, wrapped in a sheet to keep warm, tears streaming down my face as I thought about everything that had just happened. After a few minutes, the door opened. It felt like my punishment was over.

I walked back into the room slowly and sat on the edge of the bed. Lonnie was at the small table, finishing the rest of the alcohol and smoking something that definitely wasn't a cigarette.

I lay back on the bed, my eyes fixed on him, my heart beating fast. The room was heavy with silence. After a moment, Lonnie stood and walked toward me. He sat down beside me, his face only inches from mine. Tears glistened on his cheeks.

"Do you love him? Do you want to be with him?" he asked, his voice cracking.

His words—and the pain behind them—shook me to my core. I had really hurt him. This man, who could make others tremble just by walking into a room, was now breaking in front of me. And it was my fault. My heart ached.

I sat up and gently touched his cheek, turning his face toward mine. "I love you," I whispered. "I want only you. That was a mistake—one I regret more than anything. I'm sorry. I'm so sorry."

I wrapped my arms around his waist and began to kiss his neck, then his cheeks. At first, he didn't respond. Then, slowly, he kissed me back.

We made love with tears in our eyes and fell asleep holding each other tight, as if we were both afraid to let go.

13

Chapter 13

Insecurities

It's been a month since I confessed to Lonnie about me and Sam, and our relationship hasn't been the same since. I find myself doing everything he asks, trying to make up for the hurt I caused. If I'm not at work, I'm with him.

We stay on the phone more than usual, but most of our time together is just me watching him and his friends smoke and drink. I sit quietly, smiling when I can, pretending everything's fine. But I can feel myself shrinking—back into that girl from Arkansas who always fell in line, never spoke up, just wanted to please everyone.

"Can I get everyone's attention?" A strong voice pulled me out of my thoughts. I almost forgot I was at work.

I turned toward the supervisor, who was walking to the back where all the staff had gathered. "Today is Mrs. Janice's birthday, so let's wish her a happy birthday!"

We all cheered and sang, some off-key, which made Mrs. Janice laugh. I tried to smile, but I wasn't really feeling up to it. I'd felt sick all day. The smell of chicken-fried steak made me nauseous—I just wanted to go home.

When my shift ended, Mrs. Janice came over to where I was standing outside. "You have a phone call," she said with a knowing look.

Lonnie. Everyone already knew who it was—he'd called eight times since my shift started.

I looked down at the ground, closed my eyes, and took a breath before heading back inside.

"Hello," I said, my voice tired.

"Hey," Lonnie replied. "You're off, right? You on your way over here?" His voice had that stern edge again.

"I'm not feeling too good. I was going to go home," I said quietly.

"Get here," he snapped.

"Fine. I'll be there in a little bit."

I hung up, grabbed my things, and stepped outside. My body ached everywhere.

Mrs. Janice was still sitting out front. "Come here, let me talk to you," she said gently, in that motherly way of hers.

"Are you pregnant?"

"Pregnant? Why would you say that?" I asked, startled.

"Well, baby, over the last few weeks you've gotten bigger. You've been throwing up, and you follow that boy around like a lost puppy."

I froze. Could she be right? Am I pregnant?

As I looked at her, fear set in, and she could see it written all over my face.

"Aww, baby," she said gently. "It'll be alright. God has a plan for every one of us, and if you are pregnant, just know He'll be with you every step of the way. Just pray, baby."

She pulled me into a hug, reassuring me that everything was going to be alright.

My mind was racing as I walked all the way to Lonnie's mom's house. When I arrived, I called my mom to let her know where I was—just in case she was expecting me home after work.

I sat on the couch, holding my stomach, thinking about the possibility that I might be with child. Lonnie walked in and leaned over to kiss me. The smell of whatever was on him hit me so hard that my stomach turned. I pushed him away.

"What is that smell?" I asked.

He frowned. "What are you talking about? I don't smell like anything." He grabbed his shirt and sniffed it, then stumbled across the room toward his bag. He pulled out a bottle of alcohol, took a swig, and staggered back to the couch, flopping down beside me.

I looked at him, concern written all over my face. "Are you drunk?"

He laughed. "Nah, just had a couple drinks with Randy and the guys earlier." Then he took another sip straight from the bottle, laid his head back, and closed his eyes.

I shook my head. Yeah, he's drunk.

What am I doing? Why can't I break this hold he has over me?

I took the bottle from his hand as he started to drift off. When I stood up, the room spun. I grabbed my head and reached for the arm of the couch to steady myself.

Just then, his mother walked in. "Punkin, what's wrong with you?"

"I'm okay," I said, catching my balance and holding my stomach. "Just got dizzy—stood up too fast."

She squinted at me. "Why you holding your stomach? You pregnant?"

Her words startled me. "No, ma'am," I replied, my voice shaky and unsure.

Lonnie stirred, his eyes half-open. "Pregnant?" he mumbled. Then he smiled lazily. "My baby having my baby," he said, reaching for me before his arm dropped weakly to his side.

A flood of emotions hit me all at once. I wanted to run and hide, but instead, I just stood there, staring blankly at his mom.

"Lonnie, you need to take this child to the clinic and get a test," she said before walking off to her room.

I sat back down, silent at first. Then I whispered, "Lonnie, I want to go home."

He groaned. "Come on, girl. Let me sleep a little longer," he said, rubbing my stomach.

Tears filled my eyes as I shook him harder. "I want to go home. Now."

He didn't budge. Eventually, I closed my eyes and drifted off to sleep.

The next day, it was confirmed—I was pregnant. My heart dropped as the doctor said aloud what everyone already knew.

Excitement lit up Lonnie's face as he leaned down and kissed my forehead. But I felt

something else entirely—nervous, scared. I hid it behind a smile, I sat up and wrapped my arms around and gave him a tight hug.

It had been a couple of months since I found out I was pregnant, and it felt like my stomach had grown overnight. I lay on his mom's couch, replaying the conversation I'd had with my own mother—one that hadn't been as bad as I'd feared. Still, it was the hurt and disappointment in her eyes that I couldn't bear.

I eventually fell asleep thinking about her—about the way she held me and told me that everything was going to be alright.

Boom. Boom. Boom.

The hard knocking yanked me out of a peaceful sleep.

I looked over to where Lonnie should've been lying, but the spot was empty.

"Hold on, I'm coming," I called, rolling out of bed to answer the door.

When I peeked out the window, I saw who it was—his mom, her arms full of grocery bags.

"Where that boy at? He need to come get the rest of these groceries out the car," she said, a cigarette hanging from her mouth.

"I don't know. He wasn't here when I woke up. You want me to get them?" I asked, taking some of the bags from her arms.

"Girl, if you and your big belly don't go sit down somewhere," she said, shooing me off as she headed back out the door.

I laughed softly and started putting the groceries away.

When I glanced at the clock, I realized it was almost time for my doctor's appointment—and Lonnie was still nowhere to be found.

I got dressed and started walking toward the bus stop. Halfway down the street, I saw him running out of the neighbor's house, trying to catch up to me.

A car full of guys drove by, one leaning out the window. "Hey, cutie! You need a ride?" he shouted.

Before I could say anything, Lonnie grabbed my arm. "Nah, partner, she good," he snapped, yanking me around to face him.

"Who was that? And where you going dressed like that?" he demanded.

"I don't know them," I said, my face tight with confusion. "I'm on my way to the OBGYN—like I told you. You said you were coming with me this time, but I guess you had something more important to do this morning."

"Well, I'm here now. Let's go," he said.

"No," I told him firmly. "You reek of alcohol. I'll just go by myself again."

Just then, the bus pulled up. I got on without looking back. As I found a seat, I could still see him through the window, standing there watching me.

When my appointment was nearly over, I looked at the doctor. "Can I get another picture of the ultrasound?" I asked.

"Of course," she said, smiling. "It's almost time—are you excited?"

She moved the transducer gently across my belly, searching for a good angle. "Do you want to know the sex this time?"

I hesitated. At first, I'd wanted it to be a surprise. But now, I needed to know—so I could be ready for whatever comes next.

"Yes," I said quietly. "I'd like to know." It's a girl she said.

I smiled, my heart melted on the inside with overwhelming joy.

I finally made it back to Lonnie's house, and once again, he was nowhere to be found.

I sat on the porch with his little sister.

"Hey, where's your brother?" I asked.

"He's next door, over at Kelvin's house," she said.

"Oh, okay."

I sat outside for a while, but the heat was draining, so I went inside. A few minutes later, Lonnie came in, dripping with sweat.

"What were you doing over at Kelvin's house?" I asked. "You're sweaty, and what's that smell?"

"Nothing," he said quickly. "I'm about to jump in the shower. The guys are throwing a party at the motel tonight, and I told them we'd stop by."

He kissed me on the forehead and disappeared into the bathroom.

Through the window, I could hear laughter and loud music outside, so I stepped back out to look. It was Kelvin, getting out of a car with some girl.

Then Lonnie's little sister came out and sat on their porch.

"Hey, Miss Punkin!" she said, waving in my direction.

I smiled, waved back, and went inside again.

Sitting on the couch, I couldn't shake the thought — if Kelvin's just getting home now, why did Lonnie say he was over there earlier?

Right then, Lonnie walked in, pulling on a T-shirt.
   "You wearing that, or you need to change?" he asked.

"I'm just gonna wear this," I said, trying to lift myself off the couch. "I'm gonna make me a sandwich before we leave. You want one?"

"Nah, I'm good. Just hurry up so we can catch a ride with my homeboy."

I went into the kitchen and fixed myself a quick sandwich. Before I could even take a bite, Lonnie called out, "He's here—let's go!"

The so-called "party" didn't feel like a party to me at all. It was just a bunch of Lonnie's homeboys drinking and smoking, with a few girls wearing low-cut shirts and shorts that were way too tight.

I sat in a corner near the window, trying not to inhale whatever they were smoking.

One of the guys I knew from school came up to me. He used to have a crush on my sister.
   "Hey! I haven't seen you in a while. How you been? How's your sister?" he asked.

"She's good," I said. "And me, well—" I pointed down at my stomach.

"Oh wow, congratulations! Yeah, you been busy," he said, laughing.

We both laughed and started reminiscing about our Kimball High band days.

Then Lonnie walked up.

"'Scuse me, potna," he said, his face tight with anger. "Let's go, Punkin."

Before I could react, he shoved the guy aside and grabbed my arm, yanking me to my feet.

"Lonnie, you're hurting my arm," I said, trying to pull away.

"Well get up then—let's go!" he barked, letting go suddenly.

I stood up, embarrassed, feeling every pair of eyes in the room on me. With my head lowered, I followed him out.

We crossed through the Bluitt Flowers Clinic parking lot across the street from the motel—far enough to be out of sight from the nosy crowd. Lonnie was fussing and cursing the whole way.

"So you just talk to anybody now, huh? Who was that?" he shouted, shaking me.

When he raised his hand like he was about to hit me as he did before, something in me snapped.

Not this time, I said to myself.

I let my body drop, falling to the ground. Curling up, I cried out, "Uhh!" and held my stomach, pretending I was in pain from the shaking and the shove. All I could think about was my baby.

"Oh my God! What did I do? I'm sorry—I'm sorry," he said over and over, his voice trembling.

He picked me up and carried me in his arms all the way to his mom's house, kissing my cheeks as he hurried down the street. I didn't know where his strength came from, but somehow, we made it there fast.

"Momma! Momma!" he shouted as we came through the door.

"What is it, boy?" she asked, rushing over.

"It's the baby—we need to go to the hospital!"

I sat on the couch, holding my stomach, pretending to be in pain.

"Let me get my keys," she said. "I'll take y'all."

We loaded into the car and headed to the hospital. On the way, Lonnie leaned over and whispered, "Tell them you tripped and fell."

I looked into his bloodshot eyes and nodded.

After all the tests and a sonogram, the doctor said the baby was fine. The relief on Lonnie's face was overwhelming—he looked like he wanted to cry.

As we left, his mom gave me that same talk she'd given before.
   "Girl, you need to go home and stay away from him. He ain't no good for you."

She'd taken me home once before, sat with my mom, and told her the same thing. I'd always stay away for a week or two—and then go right back.

But not this time.

This was my breaking point.

Lying on that ground, I had prayed that God would break the hold he had on me.

When we got back to the house, I looked at his mom—sadness and strength in my eyes—and said softly,

"I'm ready to go home now."

14

Chapter 14

Unexpected

Ring, ring.

I heard the telephone blaring from across the room. Ugh… I groaned. Of course, I'd left it on the dresser. Forcing myself out of bed, I shuffled across the room and grabbed the cordless receiver.

"Hello," I mumbled in my sleepy voice.

"Heeey, my big belly friend! Get up, I know you're still in that bed!"

It was Mekia. We both laughed.

"And I sure am," I said jokingly. "How are you and little baby LonMekia doing?"

"Girl, I told you I am not naming my baby that!" I laughed. "But for real, how are you doing?"

How am I doing? I thought, sinking back onto my bed and pulling the covers over me. It had been almost three weeks since I'd been over to Lonnie's house.

"I'm okay," I said, though even I could hear the doubt in my voice. "Just ready to have this baby so I can finally stretch out in this bed again." I shifted around, trying to get comfortable.

"Well, you don't have much longer to go! What is it, another week or two?"

"I know. I'm a little nervous and excited at the same time," I said, rubbing my stomach.

"Ouch!"

"What is it?" Mekia asked, her voice full of concern.

"Nothing, she just kicked me in the ribs. She's been moving a lot this morning."

"Oh girl, don't scare me like that! I thought I was gonna have to call 911 the way you hollered."

"You're crazy," I said, laughing.

"Okay girl, I'll call you later and check up on you. Love you, girlie."

"Love you too. Talk to you later, bye."

I hung up and drifted right back to sleep.

A few hours later, I woke up hungry—as usual—craving an Ultimate Cheeseburger from Jack in the Box. Normally, Lonnie would've gone to get it for me, but we hadn't really been talking much lately.

Suddenly, a sharp pain spread across my lower stomach. This didn't feel like the usual aches. I winced, then went to call the nurse line to ask what I could do for relief.

"Go to the hospital!" the nurse said firmly.

"Go to the hospital?" I repeated out loud, startled. My heart started pounding. What if something was wrong?

I hung up and quickly called Lonnie, but his sister answered.

"Hey, let your brother know I'm on my way to Parkland Hospital to get checked out. I'm in a little pain," I told her.

"Okay, I'll tell him," she said.

I tried calling a few other people for a ride but had no luck. So, I grabbed my bus pass and headed out the door. Thankfully, I didn't have to wait long—the bus was already coming up the street.

I got on and sat right behind the driver. As we stopped to pick up more passengers, I looked up and froze—Lonnie stepped on. He looked just as surprised as I felt.

"You okay?" he asked, reaching for my hand as he sat beside me. One of his friends sat in the seat in front of us.

The ride was quiet and awkward. We hadn't seen each other since the night of the party. I was nervous—partly about the baby, partly about him—but deep down, I was a little relieved he was there.

When we arrived at the ER, they sent us straight to maternity. The nurses checked my vitals; my blood pressure was high. They hooked me up to the baby monitor, and I exhaled when I heard her heartbeat—strong and steady.

Lonnie watched in awe, his eyes fixed on the monitor. Hearing his daughter's heartbeat for the first time seemed to silence everything else in the room.

The nurse checked my progress, her gloved hands gentle but precise. "You're at five centimeters," she said, glancing up with a reassuring smile. "Most likely, you'll be a new mother sometime today."

A flutter of excitement burst in my chest—tiny butterflies that wouldn't settle. The monitors beside me hummed softly, their lights blinking in quiet rhythm, like a heartbeat waiting for its cue.

"Are you in any pain?" the nurse asked.

I shook my head. "No, not really."

She frowned slightly, studying the screen. "That's strange—the monitor says you're having contractions."

"I just feel pressure," I explained. "Like I have to use the bathroom, but no pain."

Her eyes widened. "Really? These are reading as strong contractions."

I managed a small smile. "No pain, ma'am. Promise."

She looked at me in amazement, and I wondered if it was because of the metal rods in my back from the scoliosis surgery I'd had at thirteen—or maybe because of all the quiet talks I'd been having with God these past few days. Probably a little of both. Either way, I smiled to myself, feeling a calmness that could only come from Him.

The door opened, and in walked Dr. Dean, his smile bright enough to light up the room.

"Hey!" he called cheerfully. "Don't start the party without me."

We laughed, and he crossed the room to Lonnie, extending his hand. "You must be the father-to-be."

Lonnie stood, shaking his hand. "Yes, sir. That's me."

"Alright, Mama," Dr. Dean said, turning back to me. "Let's see what's going on."

He studied my chart, his brow furrowing. "Blood pressure's a little high," he murmured. Then his eyes moved to the monitor, where another contraction began to build.

"That's a big one," he said. "Are you sure you're not in pain?"

"No," I said again, steady. "Just pressure."

The nurse looked at him. "They're coming closer together now."

"Let's check her position," he said, slipping on his gloves. "And see how far along she is."

The examination made me flinch, my body tightening. I closed my eyes and exhaled a shaky breath.

"She's at eight centimeters," Dr. Dean announced. "Let's get her ready for delivery. Call the team."

"Wait—what?" My eyes flew open.

He smiled kindly. "Yes, ma'am. She's ready to meet her parents."

For a moment, everything froze. My mom and sister aren't here yet. What if something goes wrong? What if I can't do this? My heart raced as nerves and excitement tangled inside me.

I looked at Lonnie—he looked just as nervous as I felt.

"You both have nothing to worry about," Dr. Dean said gently. "You and your baby are in good hands."

Just then, the door swung open and my mom walked in, followed by his mom and sister. Relief washed through me like a tide pulling away the fear. Surrounded by love, I finally felt ready—ready to meet the little soul who'd already changed my life.

"What white man you been with?" Mekia laughed, her voice teasing as she cradled my baby girl in her arms.

I rolled my eyes, grinning despite myself. My daughter's skin was lighter than mine, her tiny eyelids fluttering in sleep. Her eyes—when they were open—were a soft gray, with a hint of brown that caught the light like honey.

"Stop it," I said, pressing a hand to my stomach. "Don't make me laugh—it still hurts. I've only been home for three weeks."

I tossed a receiving blanket at her, half in play, half in warning. The laundry basket at my feet overflowed with onesies and tiny socks, each one smelling faintly of baby powder and detergent.

"For real though," Mekia said, her tone softening. "She's beautiful. Has Lonnie been coming by? I know it's been… weird since y'all broke up."

I sighed, folding a tiny pink shirt. "He visits when he can, but it's been a while.

He keeps asking me to bring the baby by, but I don't know. You remember how I was—it's like he had some kind of hold on me. And I can't—no, I won't—go through that again. It was toxic. Once I asked God to bring me out of that situation, I promised myself I'd never go back."

I stared down at the pile of clothes, lost for a moment in the rhythm of folding. "But I do miss his family. His mom, his sister, his brothers... I know they want to meet her."

Mekia nodded, rocking the baby gently. "Whatever you decide, make sure it's your choice. Don't let what people think push you one way or another. This is your life. And you know I got your back."

"Thanks, girl." I leaned over to hug her, careful not to wake the little bundle nestled against her chest.

"I'll take her," I said, reaching out. The baby stirred as I laid her in the bassinet, her lips parting in a tiny sigh. I stood there for a moment, just watching her breathe.

Then I turned to Mekia. "You know what? Maybe I will take her to see his family. Will you ride with me?"

"Of course," she said, smiling. "You know I got you."

"I shouldn't let what happened between me and him stop me from seeing them," I said quietly, more to myself than to her. "I'm stronger now."

I grabbed the diaper bag and began to pack, my hands steady this time. "I'll call his mom and let her know we'll be stopping by."

We arrived later that evening.

"Oh, look who came to visit their granny!" Miss Gertie called out as I unbuckled the baby from her car seat.

Before I could even lift her out, all the kids came running from the house, crowding around the car, trying to catch a glimpse of the new baby.

"Can I hold her?" Lonnie's sister asked as I made my way up the porch, carefully carrying the car seat.

"Sure," I said, smiling. "But be careful—"

Before she could finish unstrapping her, Miss Gertie swooped in. "Me first!" she said, scooping the baby up into her arms.

"Aww, she got eyes just like Lonnie when he was a baby. They gon' turn hazel—his did the same thing. Punkin, she's gorgeous." Her face lit up with pride, a smile stretching from ear to ear.

That's when Lonnie walked in. Handsome as ever.

"Hey," he said, giving a small nod.

I nodded back, unsure of what to say. He stood there for a moment, eyes locked on mine, like he wanted to speak—but before he could, a soft whimper filled the room.

He turned toward his mother. "Can I please have my child?" he asked, grinning playfully.

Miss Gertie laughed and handed the baby over.

"Hello, my sweet little girl," he said softly. "It's Daddy."

The moment froze—him holding her close, the room quiet except for the sound of her breathing. He lingered there, rocking her gently, before looking around for a place to sit. The only empty spot was next to me.

He sat down carefully, both of us pretending not to notice how close we were.

"You smell good," he murmured.

I didn't know if he meant me or the baby. Our eyes met—those same eyes I'd fallen in love with years ago—and for a second, it felt like nothing had changed.

"I got something for her," he said, breaking the silence.

He handed the baby back to me and disappeared into the back room. When he returned, he held a pink porcelain piggy bank and a small stack of twenties.

"We need to talk," he said, handing me the money.

Before I could answer, a horn blared outside—beep, beep.

He glanced toward the door. "I gotta go handle something. Can you stay here till I get back?"

I hesitated. "...Yeah."

He smiled, leaned in, and pressed a kiss to my forehead. "I love you," he whispered before hurrying out the door.

I stood there, holding our daughter, watching through the window as he climbed into the car with his friends.

Time passed. Mekia had left hours ago, and I was still waiting—waiting to see what any of it meant. I drifted off on the couch, the baby asleep on my chest.

The ringing phone jolted me awake. It was after one in the morning.

Miss Gertie answered. "Hello?"

A pause. Then her voice broke—
   "What? He was shot?"
   sat up quickly, waiting for her to say who. But Miss Gertie was still on the phone, her voice trembling as she spoke to whoever was on the other end. My stomach dropped; my heart was racing.

When she finally turned to me, tears streaking her face, her voice cracked.
   "Lonnie's been shot. They're taking him to Parkland."

My heart sank. I stared at the door, frozen, wondering if that was the last time I'd ever see him alive.

His sister moved fast, grabbing the baby and snapping her into the car seat. "Let's go, Punkin! Come on!" she yelled over her shoulder as she headed out the door.

I slipped on my shoes as I ran, barely able to breathe.

When we burst into the hospital, the fluorescent lights felt too bright, the air too heavy. We rushed to the front desk. "I'm looking for my—" she started, but a voice cut her off.

"Gertie!"

One of Lonnie's friends was standing down the hallway, his face pale, eyes red. The rest of his crew sat slumped in the waiting room. We hurried toward him.

"What's going on?" she demanded.

"They took him to surgery," he said quietly. "The doctor said he'll update us once they're done. We've just been waiting."

As we moved toward the waiting area, she asked the question we were all thinking. "What happened?"

Randy's voice shook. "We were at the trap. Lonnie was laying on the floor in front of the TV with his gun, wrapped up in a blanket... and it went off." He paused, his eyes darting around. "We didn't think nothing of it at first—he's always messing with that gun—but then we heard him moaning, rolling around on the floor..."

The story didn't sound right. It felt rehearsed. I kept listening, but inside, something told me there was more. Gertie's face said the same. She didn't believe it either.

Just then, the surgeon walked into the waiting room.

"Are you his mother?" he asked.

"Yes," Gertie said, clutching her purse to her chest.

"We have your son in a medically induced coma," the doctor explained. "We need to reduce the swelling before we can remove the remaining bullet fragments. If you'll come with me, I can explain more."

Gertie reached for my hand. Together we followed him down the ICU hallway, her daughter trailing behind us with the baby in her arms.

When we reached the room, there was a glass window just before the door. I looked through—and my heart stopped.

Lonnie lay there, his head swollen to nearly three times its size, tubes coming out from everywhere. The bullet had entered through his cheek and exited through his head, leaving fragments scattered around his brain.

My legs gave out. I hit the floor, sobbing uncontrollably. Nurses rushed to help, lifting me into a chair, but I couldn't stop shaking.

Gertie went into the room, but I couldn't bring myself to follow. I just sat there, rocking, thinking about the last words he said to me.

I love you.

And I never said it back.

Why didn't I say it back?

Somewhere in the background, I heard the baby crying. The sound felt far away, until I realized it wasn't—it was right there. A nurse was trying to soothe her but couldn't. I reached out, and she placed the baby in my arms. I held her close, crying silently until she fell asleep against my chest.

We came back the next day. And the day after that. No change.

A week later, the doctors said they were going to take him off life support—to see if he could breathe on his own.

That morning, we all gathered in the room. The air was thick with fear. No one spoke. The nurse pressed a button, and the steady hum of the machine began to fade.

I held my breath and closed my eyes, praying for a miracle.

Then—beep.

The monitor came alive again.

"He's still with us!" Gertie cried.

Lonnie's chest rose and fell, faint but steady. Joy and relief washed over me. I grabbed his hand, squeezed it tight, whispering that I was there. His mother held his other hand.

For the first time in days, things felt like they were finally turning around.

That night, I went home. I was just settling in when the phone rang.

It was Gertie. Her voice broke before she even spoke.

"Punkin... he didn't make it."

The words hung in the air, heavy and unreal. I didn't respond right away—couldn't. My chest tightened as the meaning slowly sank in. He's gone.

"We have to get going if you want to make it to Gertie's before the family car leaves," my mom said, already packing the baby bag. She glanced around the room, checking for anything we might have forgotten. "I know she really wanted you and the baby to ride."

I nodded, moving on instinct alone. Black clothes. Diapers. A blanket. Somewhere between the phone call and the zipper of the bag, I realized there was no avoiding it anymore. This was real.

I sat on the edge of the bed, numb, staring into space. It was kind of her to come help me get ready—especially today, one of the hardest days of my life.

My relationship with my mom felt different. Ever since she moved out last year and left the apartment to me and my sister, we didn't spend much time together anymore. I worried about her—especially after she ended the relationship she had been in. Now she filled her days with double shifts at the hospital, working nonstop so she wouldn't have to go home to an empty place.

I watched her move around the room, folding blankets and checking bottles, and couldn't help but think about how much had changed between us.
    "Okay, Mama," I said softly, forcing a small smile.

Another tear slipped down my cheek. I looked at her, wanting to say, I don't think I can do this, but the words wouldn't come.

I slid my feet into my shoes and bent down to fasten them. Everything felt like it was happening in slow motion—the air heavy, my body weak.

"Mom," I said quietly, "can you call and let them know we'll just meet them at the church instead? I don't think I'm strong enough."

She gave me a gentle nod. "Okay, baby," she said, and left the room to grab the phone.

I walked over to the bassinet and lifted Londra into my arms. She was so small, so peaceful. I stared down at her, remembering one of the last conversations her father and I had—the real reason we broke up.
    Is she mine... or his?
    That was the conversation we had right before your birth.
    He thought the only reason I didn't want to be in a relationship with him anymore was because of the timing—when you were conceived. He never considered the bruises, the fear, the way love had begun to hurt. Everything

always circled back to Sam. I told him I wasn't sure. But I told him I loved him. And he loved me. And you.

I thought about that conversation as I sat in the pew.

The church was packed—every pew filled, people standing along the walls and spilling into the aisles. It showed just how deeply he was loved.

The family lined up to walk in. My legs trembled, my heart pounding so loud I could hear it in my ears. As we made our way down the aisle, all eyes were on us.

His mother walked ahead, trying to stay composed, her face hidden beneath the black veil attached to her hat. But even through it, I could see the tears falling.

Keep it together, Punkin, I whispered to myself over and over as we drew closer to the casket.

I sat in the front row with the immediate family, holding Londra tightly in my arms. Throughout the entire service, I couldn't bring myself to look at the casket. I just stared straight ahead, rocking my baby gently, trying to hold myself together.

Then came the part I'd been dreading since the phone call—the viewing. The final goodbye.

Row by row, people stood. Soft cries filled the sanctuary as they approached the front, some whispering prayers, others offering condolences to the family.

When it was our turn, one of the aunties reached out and took Londra from my arms. My body felt heavy as I rose to my feet.

I walked slowly toward the casket. My knees went weak when I saw him.

The scream tore out of me before I could stop it—raw, uncontrollable. Hands reached out to comfort me, but I couldn't feel them. I collapsed against the casket, sobbing, calling his name over and over.

"Lonnie!"

My world spun. Then everything went black.

15

Chapter 15

Moving Forward

When I came to, I was in the family car, rocking back and forth. The murmurs around me blurred together until I heard someone say, "Give her the baby. That'll help."

They placed Londra in my arms—crying, just like me. I held her close, pressing her tiny face to mine.

All I could think about was Lonnie—how much I loved him, how much I missed him, how unfair it all felt.

"Look, look, look—she's doing it! Come on, baby! Come on, baby girl, you can do it!"

The room filled with laughter and shouts of encouragement as my aunt and cousins cheered Londra on. She stood with her back against the wall, bouncing in excitement, clapping her tiny hands—unsure if she could leave the safety of the wall that had been holding her up.

My aunt knelt down, jingling her car keys in front of her. The sound caught Londra's attention, her eyes lighting up. Slowly, she lifted one foot, then the other.

One step.

Two steps.

She wobbled, then fell—but before anyone could move, she pushed herself back up and tried again. Determined. Brave.

And then—she made it.

The room erupted in joy. Cheers, laughter, and tears all at once. My baby had taken her first steps.

As everyone celebrated, I found myself drifting into thought. Watching her, I saw something more than a milestone—I saw God's love reflected in her.

Through her tiny steps, He was showing me that I could take mine too. I could move forward, even from my comfort zone. I might fall, but I could always get back up—because He's right here with me, cheering me on.

He never left me, not even in my mistakes. He's protected me, wrapped me in His love every time I felt unworthy of it.

It's been months since we laid you to rest.

I looked at our daughter, her little face beaming as she clapped for herself—and I smiled through the ache in my chest.

"I'll be okay," I whispered.

"That'll be fourteen dollars and twenty-one cents," the cashier said, smiling at Londra, who was busy playing with one of her toys in the grocery cart.

"What's her name? She's a cutie," the cashier added.

"Londra—but we call her Shay," I replied, digging through the diaper bag for my wallet. Before I could find it, a voice beside me said, "I got it," and handed the cashier a twenty-dollar bill.

I looked up. OMG—Sam!

I stared at him, then at the cashier, then back at him. "You don't have to do that. I've got it," I said softly.

"It's fine," he said, brushing it off.

The cashier handed him his change with a smile that lingered too long. "You have a nice day," she said in a flirty tone, her eyes trailing over him.

"Thanks," I muttered, grabbing my bags and placing them in the cart. I started pushing toward the door. Sam thanked the cashier, his eyes never leaving me, and followed.

"So... this is your baby?" he asked, glancing down at Shay, studying her face as if searching for something familiar. "When's her birthday?"

The question hit me like a punch. My stomach tightened. Why is he asking that?

"Why?" I asked, pushing the cart a little faster toward the car where my cousin was waiting.

He reached out, stopping the cart. Looking straight into my eyes, he asked the question that had haunted me for months.

"Is she mine?"

I lifted Shay out of the cart, clutching the grocery bags in one hand. Looking into his curious light brown eyes, the words slipped out before I could stop them.

"I don't know."

And it was true. The same answer I'd given Lonnie when he'd asked me, too.

"You okay, cuz?" my cousin called, stepping out of the car.

"I'm fine," I said quickly, opening the back door to load the bags and buckle Shay into her car seat.

"Okay," he said, getting back in.

Sam caught my arm before I could close the door. "We need to talk about this, don't you think?"

"Really?" I snapped. "You've been back in town for months. Why now? If you really cared, you would've come by the house." I pulled my arm away and climbed into the car. "Just leave me alone, Sam. Bye."

As we pulled off, I looked into the side mirror. Sam stood there in the parking lot, watching us go, and my heart sank with a grief I couldn't name.

He never cared enough to reach out, I thought, remembering the same painful conversation I'd had with Lonnie.

"You're going to have to talk to him eventually, cuz," my cousin said quietly.

"I know," I whispered. "But not today. Not today."

I looked down at the small bushel of flowers lying in the cup holder—the ones I'd bought earlier that morning.

"Today's his birthday," I said, staring out the window as tears blurred my vision. I thought about Lonnie—and the ache in my chest deepened.

"Seven-thirty, huh? He's late—as usual," I muttered to myself, glancing up at the clock while tidying the living room. "He's the one who wanted to talk. After begging for two weeks, I finally agreed… and he's late." If it wasn't for my sweet baby girl, we wouldn't be having a conversation.

A soft knock at the door made my stomach twist. My legs felt shaky as I walked over and opened it.

There he was—Sam—looking even better than I remembered, smelling incredible, and holding a bouquet of roses. He still gave me butterflies.

"Hey," I said, trying to sound calm. "Come in, but be quiet. Shay's sleeping."

"Okay," he replied, stepping inside and closing the door behind him. He walked over to the sofa where I sat.

"I brought these for you," he said, leaning down to hand me the roses.

"They're beautiful," I said, lifting them to my nose. "Thank you. I'll put them in some water later. Have a seat."

I gestured for him to sit across from me, but Sam—being Sam—sat right next to me instead.

He took my hand and looked me straight in the eyes. "Look," he began softly, "I've been trying to say this for weeks. I'm sorry I didn't come see you sooner.

When I found out you had a kid, I was… in my feelings. I was hurt. But then I saw a picture of her—and I knew she wasn't that other guy's child. She's mine."

His eyes searched mine, silently begging for confirmation.

"Sam," I said quietly, "I can't tell you she's yours… because I don't know for sure."

"But there's a possibility, right?" he asked, a flicker of hope in his voice.

I nodded. "Yes, Sam. There's a possibility."

That was all he needed to hear.

"Can I see her?" he asked, his voice trembling slightly.

"Okay," I said softly. "But be quiet—I just put her down."

He followed me down the hall to Shay's room. We stood in the doorway, watching her sleep peacefully.

"She's so beautiful," he whispered. "Even in her sleep."

I glanced at him. The look on his face—the softness in his eyes—told me everything. In his heart, he already believed she was his.

He reached over and wrapped his arms around me, and then he began to cry. My heart melted—feeling the weight of his emotions, the love he already had for a child he'd only just met. Oh, how I still love this man.

I put my arms around him, wanting to comfort him. After a moment, he lifted his head from my shoulder. Our eyes met, and before I could think, our lips touched. His lips were still soft—just like I remembered. The kiss deepened, and for a brief moment, I let my mind drift back to what once was.

Then Shay stirred and made a small sound.

I pulled away, touching my lips, staring at Sam in silence before walking over to check on her. She was still sleeping.

"Is she okay?" he asked softly.

"Yeah," I whispered. "She's fine—must've been dreaming."

I turned back toward him. "I think you should go."

He stood up and caught my arm. "What if I don't?"

"This can't happen, Sam." I gently pulled free and started down the hall toward the front door. He followed behind me.

When I opened the door, I looked at him one last time. "Goodnight, Sam."

He hesitated, then turned back, his hand brushing the hem of my shirt. "You sure you don't want me to stay?"

My body screamed yes, but my heart wasn't sure.

"Goodnight, Sam," I repeated softly.

He sighed. "Okay then... goodnight. Can I at least see Shay tomorrow?"

"We'll be at the park around three. You can meet us there."

"Bet," he said, a small smile tugging at his lips. "I'll be there. See you tomorrow."

"Okay… bye."

"Bye."

When the door closed behind him, I leaned against it, my heart racing—wondering what might have happened if he'd stayed.

Then I heard Shay crying softly in the distance, and it pulled me back to reality.
"Mommy's coming," I whispered, pushing off the door and walking toward her room.

Old feelings resurfaced, memories of what we once were flooding my mind. I lifted Shay into my arms and rocked her gently, swaying back and forth as I sang Pretty Brown Eyes by Mint Condition.

"You want to build a sandcastle? Let's build a sandcastle," I said, smiling as Shay and I began patting sand into cups and buckets.

"Wow! What a nice castle."

I looked up, shielding my eyes from the sun with my hand. It was Sam.

"But I bet I can make one even better," he teased, kicking off his shoes and stepping into the sandbox. He sat down next to Shay and began helping her build another castle.

They looked so natural together—so comfortable. Shay giggled as she poured sand on Sam's arm, and he made a silly face, sending her into even more laughter.

I couldn't help but smile, watching the two of them play.

Then Sam glanced up at me, a soft smile tugging at his lips. "Thank you," he whispered.

I smiled back and nodded.

He reached over and took my hand gently. "You know I still love you, right?"

A rush of emotions washed over me—confusion, longing, and the ache of something I'd never really let go of. But hearing those words was exactly what my heart had been craving.

I looked into his eyes and whispered, "I still love you too."

16

Chapter 16

Be Careful For What You Wish For

Years passed, and on the surface, it seemed like the love I'd asked God for was finally unfolding in its own time. But now I understand what they mean when they say, be careful what you ask for — you just might get it.

Wake up, Mommy! Wake up!"

I slowly opened my eyes to see my two beautiful daughters tugging at my arm, giggling as they tried to pull me out of bed.

"I'm up, I'm up," I mumbled in a groggy voice. "Where's your dad?"

"He's feeding baby brother in the kitchen," one of them said.

"Okay, I'll be there in a minute."

The girls ran off, their laughter echoing down the hallway. I sighed and pulled the pillow over my head.

"Ugh, it's too early," I muttered to myself. My body felt heavy. I'd worked late yesterday, came home, cooked dinner, tidied up, and got the kids to bed. All I wanted was one morning to sleep in.

I stared up at the ceiling fan, watching it spin in slow, endless circles. Is this really my life now?

Dragging myself out of bed, I made my way to the shower. Afterward, I wiped the steam from the mirror and stared at my reflection. "Let's get this day started," I whispered to myself.

When I walked into the kitchen, it looked like a hurricane had passed through. Dirty dishes piled high in the sink.

"What happened in here?" I asked, frowning.

Sam turned from the counter, baby in one arm and bottle in the other. "I made breakfast. Your plate's on the stove."

I walked over, picked up the plate, and sat down at the table. The girls were on the floor, playing with their dolls, toys scattered everywhere across the living room.

Didn't I just clean this up last night? I thought.

"Girls," I said, trying to sound patient, "it's time to straighten up. Pick up your toys and put away the ones you're not playing with, okay?"

"They're fine," Sam said, lifting the baby from his high chair. "I'll get it later."

But I knew he wouldn't. He never did. I'd be the one cleaning up—again. Too tired to argue, I just nodded.

Sam carried the baby to the back to get him changed.

"I meant to ask you," I called out, "how did your interview go?"

"What?" he shouted back.

"Your interview! The one your homeboy set up for you."

"Oh, yeah," he said after a pause. "You know how they are—they said they'll call when they have something available."

"I thought you said it was a sure thing."

"Well... I guess they hired somebody else before the interview. I don't know."

I closed my eyes and took a slow breath, biting my tongue so I wouldn't say what I really wanted to.

"Okay," I said softly, trying to keep my tone gentle. But inside, I was screaming: Get a job, Sam. Please. Help me.

I pushed my plate away and rested my head on the table.

"This can't be my life," I whispered to myself.
  I got up and started cleaning the kitchen. Sam walked in holding the baby.

"Oh, I was going to do that," he said.

Yeah right, I thought to myself.

"It's fine, I got it," I said with a smile.

He leaned in, kissed me softly on the lips, and said, "Okay," before going to sit on the floor to play with the kids.

I shook my head and kept cleaning, glancing over at him from time to time. Watching him with the kids made me smile. He really was a great dad. He loved them, and they loved him.

"Thank you for calling 1-800-Flowers, how can I help you?"

"Girl, you still coming to the party I'm throwing for my man tonight, right?" my friend Tasha said, standing on the side of my cubicle.

"May I place you on a brief hold? Thank you," I said into the phone before covering the receiver. "You see I'm on a call, right?" I whispered, giving her a look.

"Girl, forget those people! I'm trying to tell you how lit this party's gonna be," she said, snapping her fingers and dancing in place.

I laughed. "Yes, I'm coming. Sam's staying with the kids. Now let me do my job before you get me fired."

"Okay, okay! We'll talk later," she said, walking off.

As soon as I hung up, Tasha popped right back over, grinning ear to ear, ready to tell me every detail of the party plans. I was nervous, honestly. I didn't go out much—barely ever. The only time I'd been to a club, I sat at the table watching everyone's purses while they danced and got drunk. I always felt a little awkward in those settings.

"Okay, girl," Tasha said as she left for the day, "I'm picking you up around eight-thirty."

"Okay, sounds great! I'll be ready," I said, though I had no idea what I was going to wear.

When I got home, I rushed straight to the bedroom, trying to think of something—anything—I could put on. Then I saw it: a pair of pleather shorts and a top laid out neatly on the bed.

Sam appeared in the doorway, smiling. "You like it?"

I picked it up, surprised. "You got this for me?"

"Yeah," he said, grinning. "I knew you didn't have anything to wear out. And let's be real—you wouldn't know how to dress for the club."

He chuckled, and I couldn't help but laugh too. "Thank you," I said with a smile.

I jumped in the shower, then tried to squeeze into the outfit. It clung to me like plastic wrap.

"Sam!" I called.

He came running. "What's up?"

"Can you help me get this on?"

He laughed and helped me tug the top into place. "Dang, girl," he said, looking me up and down, "I don't know if I want you to go anywhere."

"Why? What's wrong?"

"Nothing—you look good."

I smiled, the compliment instantly calming my nerves.

Beep beep.

"She's here," I said, my stomach tightening.

Sam looked at me and said, "Go have fun—but not too much."

As I started toward the door, he grinned. "Dang, can I get a kiss first?"

I turned back, smiled, and kissed him before saying goodbye to the kids.

"You ready, girl?" Tasha said as we pulled up to her house so she could finish getting ready—and pick up her man before heading to the surprise party.

"I guess," I said nervously.

We got out and went inside.

"Now, where does he think we're going again?" I asked.

"Out to eat with some friends," she said, grinning. "Now don't you get in there and ruin the surprise."

I laughed. "Girl, I'm just playing. I know better."

We both laughed as she offered me something to drink.

"No, thank you. I'm good," I said.

Tasha dashed to the back to get ready and check on her man. I sat on the couch, wondering what Sam and the kids were doing.

A few minutes later, they came from the back together.

"Mike, this is my homegirl, Punkin," Tasha said.

"Nice to meet you," he said. "Y'all ready to go?"

"Yeah, let me grab my cup out the fridge," Tasha said, walking over to get her drink. She and Mike already seemed a little tipsy.

Lord, watch over me—and whoever's driving tonight, I thought as we headed to the car.

When we pulled into the club parking lot, it was packed.

"What we doing here?" Mike asked, looking confused.

"Surprise!" Tasha shouted. "Your boys rented out a section for us! Come on, baby—it's your night!"

Mike grinned, flashing his gold grill. "Thank you, baby," he said as he got out of the car.

We walked inside. The music was loud, the lights were dim, and the air smelled like smoke and liquor.

"Surprise!" everyone yelled.

"Ayy!" Mike cheered, throwing his hands in the air, dancing to the music.

Shots were being poured left and right. There was so much food, so much alcohol—Tasha really went all out for him.

But me? I felt completely out of place.

The night dragged on, and before I knew it, it was one in the morning. That's when I heard yelling from across the room.

I stood up to see Tasha holding Mike back.

"Bro, you don't know me! I'll kill you!" Mike shouted, stumbling toward a guy who'd been flirting with Tasha earlier.

Guess he found out, I thought, walking closer.

Tasha shoved her purse into my hands. "Here, take my keys—we gotta go!"

She was trying to pull Mike out of the club, but he kept yelling, "Where my gun at?!"

Gun?! Lord, what have I gotten myself into? I thought as my heart started to race.

His homeboys finally managed to get him into the car, and we drove off, their cars following behind us.

When we pulled up at Tasha's place, I asked nervously, "Umm... so you're not taking me home?"

"I'll take you in the morning, girl," she said. "I gotta get him to bed."

Her friends helped drag his limp body out of the car and down the hallway into the bedroom.

"Take his drunk butt back there," Tasha said, shaking her head.

When she came back, she handed me a T-shirt and some shorts. "Here you go, girl. Sorry about my crazy man—he had too much to drink. Everything just went left."

"It's okay, I understand," I said softly. "Can I use your phone? I need to call Sam."

"Sure—it's on the counter."

I dialed. "Hello? Hey, it's me. Tasha's man got too drunk, so we came back to her place. She said she'll take me home in the morning, okay?"

"Yeah, whatever," he said flatly.

"I love—" I started, but the line went dead.

I stared at the phone. Did he just hang up on me?

I walked into the house, bracing myself for whatever Sam had to say about me staying out all night.

He was sitting on the couch, watching TV with the kids. When he heard me come in, he turned and stared—his eyes slowly scanning me from head to toe, studying me like I was some kind of puzzle he was trying to solve.

"That's not how you were dressed when you left," he said.

"What are you talking about?" I asked, frowning.

He stood up and walked toward me, his tone sharp. "Your shorts are on wrong."

He said it with a smirk, like he'd just caught me doing something dirty.

"Again—what are you talking about?" I said, confused and uneasy.

"Yeah, okay," he said, nodding. "I heard that guy in the background—that's why you didn't come home, huh? Yeah, uh-huh." He kept repeating it over and over, his voice getting louder each time.

"Please, stop, Sam," I begged. "There was no guy. I didn't do anything."

"You gonna stand there and lie to my face?" he shouted, his voice shaking with anger. His face turned red, his eyes bloodshot.

Before I could respond, he grabbed a fistful of my hair and yanked me toward the hallway, his grip on my arm tightening.

"Sam, you're hurting me!" I cried.

He didn't answer. Instead, he threw open the closet door and shoved me inside. I lunged for the handle, but he slammed it shut and wedged a chair against it.

"Don't even think about coming out," he growled.

I froze, heart pounding. I was scared and confused—too afraid to move, too shocked to speak.

"Sam, stop! Open the door!" I cried, but he didn't answer.

I slid down to the floor, shaking, crying. My voice broke as I whispered to myself, Why is this happening to me?

The door finally opened.

Sam stood in front of me, staring, his hands balled into tight fists—like he wanted to hit me. I pleaded with him, told him I loved him. He didn't respond. He pulled me up forcefully and led me to the bedroom without saying a word.

He had already fed the kids and put them to sleep before getting me out of the closet—so they wouldn't witness daddy hurting mommy.

He threw me onto the bed and tore my clothes from my body, forcing himself on me. The more I fought, the tighter his grip became, until my bruised body finally gave up. I cried in silence, terrified of waking the kids. I couldn't believe what was happening. Someone who said he loved me—who promised he would never hurt me—was doing the exact opposite.

Afterward, he wrapped his arm tightly around me, as if afraid I might leave in the middle of the night, and fell asleep. I lay there for hours, crying, replaying everything that had just happened.

17

Chapter 17

Love Bombing

The next day I sat in silence, carefully parting my daughter's hair, the rhythmic motion of the comb doing little to quiet my thoughts. The scene from a few days ago kept replaying in my mind like a film I couldn't stop. How could he? And now, he was walking around as if nothing had happened—like everything was fine.

"Hey, my beautiful babies!" His voice cut through the quiet. The kids turned to him, their faces lighting up the room.

"How about we go to Chuck E. Cheese tonight?"

Their squeals filled the air. "Chuck E! Chuck E! Chuck E!" they chanted, bouncing with excitement. He laughed and joined in, jumping around with them, their laughter colliding into a moment that looked—on the outside—like happiness.

Then he came up behind the couch where I sat. His hands found my arms, his grip gentle this time, urging me to join in their joy.

I flinched. My skin still remembered his hands from that morning—how tightly they'd held me, how much it had hurt. The bruises, hidden beneath my sleeves, throbbed beneath his touch.

I forced a smile. The children were watching. I couldn't let them see the truth trembling beneath the surface. He kissed my cheek, a gesture that burned more than it comforted, before returning to his performance of fatherly delight.

As their laughter echoed through the house, a thought crept in. Where is this money coming from all of a sudden?

I rose quietly and checked my purse. My heart sank at the sight of my empty wallet. The air left my lungs in a shudder.

I stumbled into the bathroom, clutching the sink for balance as the tears came. My reflection stared back at me—a woman I barely recognized. My lips moved, but no sound came out. Only silent prayers filled the space between the sobs.

Work was the last place I wanted to be. The chatter of coworkers, the endless ringing phones—it all blurred into background noise as my thoughts drifted back home. I answered calls on autopilot, my voice calm and polite while my mind screamed somewhere else entirely.

I glanced at the clock on my screen. Five o'clock, finally. I grabbed my bag and rushed out the door to pick up the kids.

Sitting in the car line, I let my thoughts wander. Sam left every morning now—but where was he really going? Was he out looking for work, or doing something else?

The car door opened suddenly, pulling me from my thoughts.

"Mommy!" the kids shouted, their faces beaming.

"Hey, my babies! How was your day?"

"Good!" they chimed together.

"That's great. I was thinking we could have spaghetti for dinner. How does that sound?"

Cheers erupted from the backseat. Their excitement made me smile. I caught their faces glowing in the rearview mirror, and for a moment, everything felt lighter.

We got home with a few grocery bags for dinner. As I stepped through the door, I saw Sam.

"I'll call you back later," he said into the phone before hanging up.

"Well, what do we have here? Let me help you with those bags," he said, rushing over.

"Mommy's making spaghetti!" the kids announced.

"Oh yeah? Sounds good. Mommy's a great cook, huh?" he teased, smiling at them.

"Yeah!" they shouted, spinning and laughing around the kitchen.

I interrupted their dancing with a laugh. "Alright, you guys—go get changed and washed up. I'll make you a snack before dinner."

"Okay, Mommy!" they said before running off.

I started putting the groceries away, and Sam began helping beside me.

"You want me to make them a sandwich?" he asked.

"Sure, that would be great," I said quietly.

He hummed along to a song playing on the radio, moving around the kitchen like everything was normal. Who is this person? I thought. Then he leaned over, pressed a soft kiss against my cheek, and said, "I love you," before calling for the kids to come eat.

My eyes widened in surprise. He danced over to the table, setting down their plates with a smile. For a moment, it felt like old times—when laughter filled the house, and happiness didn't feel so fragile.

"Dinner was great," Sam said, his eyes following me as I cleared the table.

I glanced over my shoulder, gave him a small smile, and nodded. "Thanks."

"I got this," he said, standing abruptly. He began gathering the plates before I could protest. "You go relax. I'll clean the kitchen."

"Okay," I murmured, too drained to argue.

I made my way to the bedroom, each step feeling heavier than the last. The quiet of the house wrapped around me as I turned on the bath. Steam rose, curling softly through the air as I poured in lavender bubbles and a handful of Epsom salt. The water was nearly scalding—just how I liked it.

I sank into the tub, the heat soothing every ache. My eyes drifted shut, my thoughts floating somewhere between exhaustion and calm. Then—click.

The lights went out. For a second, I froze. Then a soft glow flickered in the corner of the room—a single candle lighting the darkness.

It was Sam.

"I thought you might like some company," he said gently, stepping closer. The warm candlelight danced across his skin.

He placed the candle on the edge of the tub and tested the water with his foot. "Dang, girl," he laughed, drawing it back. "Does it have to be that hot?"

A quiet laugh escaped me, the first in what felt like forever.

He eased himself in behind me, the water rippling as his arms slipped around my waist. I felt his chest rise and fall against my back, his breath brushing softly against my neck.

For a while, neither of us spoke. The silence between us wasn't heavy—it was fragile, almost healing. Then he whispered, voice low and steady, the words I had longed to hear. Promises. Apologies. Love.

His hands traced slow, gentle circles along my arms, as though trying to rewrite every bruise, every hurt. I leaned back against him, closing my eyes, letting the warmth of the water and his touch melt the walls I had built.

In that moment, I remembered us—before the shouting, before the fear. Just two people who once loved each other deeply.

And for that moment, I let myself believe in it again.

Months passed, and it seemed like everything was finally back to normal.

"Go put your shoes on," I told the kids. Their laughter filled the room as they scrambled to get ready.

"Sam, I'm taking the kids outside to play for a while!" I called out from the living room. No response.

I frowned and walked down the hall. "Did you hear—" I stopped mid-sentence. Laughter—his laughter—came from the bathroom.

I froze. Then, quietly, I stepped closer.

"I enjoyed your company yesterday," his voice said softly. "You coming tomorrow before work? Bet. Okay... see you then. Love you."

CHAPTER 17

Love you.

The words hit me like a punch to the chest. My breath caught. My heart sank so low I thought I might collapse right there in the hallway.

I turned and walked back to the living room, my legs trembling, forcing my face into something calm—something normal.

"Sam!" I called, my voice steady though my insides were shaking.

"Yeah?" he answered, sounding casual, cheerful even.

"The kids want you to take them to the park," I said.

"Okay, here I come," he replied, appearing from the back room with a smile, like nothing was wrong.

"You okay?" he asked. "I thought you were going to take them."

"I'm not feeling up to it," I said, rubbing my temple. "My head's starting to hurt. I think I'll just take something and rest while you're gone."

He nodded. "Alright, get some rest." Turning to the kids, he said, "You guys ready?"

"Yeah!" they cheered.

He leaned in, kissed me on the cheek, and smiled before heading out the door with them.

I held my breath until I heard the car pull away. Then I walked to the window and watched as they disappeared down the street. My chest tightened, a storm building inside me that I couldn't hold back much longer.

I turned toward the bedroom, picked up the phone, and pressed redial.

"Hello?"

I didn't say anything at first—just listened to the voice on the other end.

"Hello? Is anyone there?"

She doesn't know this number.

Then I glanced at the phone screen. There was a *67 before the number. He'd been blocking his calls. My stomach turned.

"I'm hanging up now," the voice said.

"No, wait!" I blurted out before she could. "Do you... do you know someone named Sam?"

There was a pause. "Yeah," she said slowly. "That's my man. Why?"

I swallowed hard. "I just hit redial on our home phone. He called you—from here. From our house. With our kids in the next room."

"What?" Her voice rose, sharp with shock. "I—I didn't know! He told me he stayed with his sister. I've never been to his place. Sometimes I pick him up, or he borrows my car while I'm at work. I swear, I didn't know about you."

My throat tightened. "It's okay," I said quietly. "I don't blame you. It's him."

I hung my head, fury and heartbreak mixing inside me until I could barely breathe. I'm sick of this, I thought. So sick of it.

Just then, the front door opened.

"Hey, we're back," Sam called out cheerfully. "The park was blocked off for repairs."

His footsteps grew closer. I stood frozen, the phone still in my hand. My heart pounded so hard I could hear it in my ears.

"Who you on the phone with?" he asked playfully as he stepped into the doorway.

"Oh, just someone who might know you," I said, my voice trembling with anger. "What's your name again?" I asked into the phone.

"Keisha," the woman said softly.

"Oh, Keisha," I repeated, staring straight at Sam. "I believe you two know each other."

I extended the phone toward him. "Here. She'd like a word."

His smile vanished. His whole face changed—cold, defensive.

"Why you on the phone with her?" he shouted, trying to snatch the phone from my hand.

"Come get him, Keisha!" I yelled, stepping back. "You can have him!"

"Give me the damn phone!" he roared, slamming it down. The argument exploded—shouting, tears, everything boiling over. The kids stood frozen in the doorway, eyes wide with fear.

I was shaking, but I'd had enough. "I'm done, Sam," I said, voice breaking. "I can't do this anymore."

Outside, I heard voices. Neighbors.

"You okay in there? Do you need the police?" someone called through the door.

Those words stopped him cold. He glanced toward the window, breathing hard, then turned and stormed out toward the parking lot.

And there she was—Keisha. Waiting

The door slammed so hard it rattled the walls.
    Then there was silence.

Just silence.

My hands were still shaking, the echo of his shouting bouncing around in my head. The phone lay on the floor, its screen cracked, the faint hum of the dial tone filling the room like a ghost.

The kids were still standing there—eyes wide, scared, confused. I forced myself to look at them, my voice breaking. "It's okay, babies... it's okay. Go to your room, please."

They hesitated, then ran down the hall, their little feet pounding against the floor.

As soon as they were gone, I sank to my knees. The weight of it all came crashing down—every lie, every bruise, every moment I convinced myself things were getting better. My chest tightened as if my heart was folding in on itself.

I pressed my hand against my mouth to muffle the sob that tore its way out. Another followed. Then another. Until I couldn't stop.

The tears came in waves, hot and endless. I curled into myself on the cold floor, shaking, gasping for air. How could he do this? After everything?

Images flashed through my mind—his smile at dinner, his laugh with the kids, the way he'd kissed me just nights ago as if we were healing. It was all a lie. Everything he'd given felt stolen.

Betrayal and anger exploded inside me. I ran to the closet and yanked out everything that belonged to him—shoes, shirts, drawers emptied, everything. I carried armfuls out into the courtyard and started throwing them up onto the apartment roof. Anything that wouldn't make it I left in a messy heap outside for anyone to take. It felt viciously good.

I came back inside and sank onto the couch, breathing hard, the taste of adrenaline still in my mouth. Then there was a knock at the door. I peered through the peephole, heart clenching—hoping it wasn't him.

It was his sister. For a second I wondered what she wanted; I didn't think twice before opening the door.

Before I knew it Sam burst in, wild-eyed, cursing as he lunged towards me, staring out the window into the yard where his things were scattered. "What the hell is this?" he shouted. I told him the rest of his stuff was on the roof.

He shoved me. I grabbed the nearest object—the leg of a kid's toy table—and swung, more to keep him off than to hurt him. The kids started screaming. His sister crouched down, trying to comfort them, hands shaking.

"You got me into this," I spat at her, fury making my voice raw. I moved toward her, but Sam stepped between us and grabbed my arms, holding me back. She kept repeating, "I didn't know he'd do this. I didn't know."

Neighbors poured out into the yard. One of them—Mrs. Anita and her son—rushed over as Sam shoved me away, pushing me to the floor. "Sam, what are you doing? You need to leave now," she shouted.

He hesitated, then turned and walked off. His sister stayed behind, trying to explain herself through tears. I wasn't very acceptive she quickly follows him out the door. The house felt hollow after they left.

The kids—wide-eyed and trembling—ran to me and wrapped their arms around my legs. I bent down and held them, my own hands still shaking. The adrenaline ebbed and left a cold, hollow ache.

How did it get this far? I thought, staring at their small faces. I swallowed hard. I had to think of them. I had to be strong for them.

18

Chapter 18

Familiar Feelings

As the years went by, the hurt you caused slowly began to fade. I tried to move on, even thought I'd found someone who could fill the empty space you left in my heart. But that marriage didn't last.

Some nights I'd sit in the living room, watching reruns of Living Single—or maybe the show was watching me. I'd drift off in a daze, surrounded by the silence of the house. The kids were all grown, with families and lives of their own, and the place just felt... still.

Every now and then, I'd see you at family gatherings your mother invited us to. You still took care of me, like old habits never died—even when you were married. I loved your two daughters you had with Keisha like they were my own. I couldn't help but smile at the way life kept circling us back together.

Then you divorced, moved on again, and had another child with someone else. Your mom would always joke, asking why you kept letting those women "steal your man." I'd laugh it off, but deep down I understood. We were two young people who fell in love too hard and too fast.

You were my first in everything. After what happened with my stepdad, I didn't think I could ever let anyone close. But you found a way to reach me. You showed me what it felt like to love—and to be loved—in a way I never thought possible.

   Buzz, buzz. The vibration of my cellphone pulled me out of my thoughts. I reached between the couch pillows and grabbed it. Before I could say a word, an excited little voice came through the line.

"Maw-Maw, you picking me up for church tomorrow?"

It was my oldest granddaughter, Miyah.

"I sure am. You ready to say your Black History speech?"

"Yes, ma'am! I'm ready."

"Alright then, I'll pick you up around seven-thirty in the morning, okay? Tell your mama."

"Okay! Love you, Maw-Maw. Bye!"

"Love you too," I said, smiling as I hung up the phone.

Spending time with my grandkids always fills me with joy—especially Miyah. Shay had her while she was still living at home, so Miyah was always around. Folks used to think she was my baby because I took her everywhere with me. The thought made me laugh.

I grabbed the remote, turned off the TV, and switched on the radio to Heaven 97. The familiar sound of gospel music filled the room as I started cooking dinner for myself.

"Dinner for one," I said to myself as I placed my plate on the table and pulled out a chair. I looked back toward the kitchen and shook my head. I should've just ordered out again.

There was so much food, and it was just me. I always cooked too much. "Someone will come by tomorrow," I said, laughing quietly. "Leftovers never stay long in this house."

As I finished eating, I reached for my laptop and started scrolling through Facebook. Then—ping—a message popped up on Messenger. It was from Sam.

"Why is it every time I'm thinking about this man, he shows up?" I muttered to myself.

Nope. I snapped the laptop shut. But curiosity got the best of me. What could he possibly want?

I opened it again slowly, like he might somehow see me through the screen. Hesitant, I clicked on the message.
   from you in a while. I miss you.

Before I could even react, the laptop started ringing. What the—? It was Sam calling me through Messenger. I didn't answer.

A few seconds later, another message popped up.
   .

"How does he—oh." I looked at my profile. The little green light was on. My son told me that meant I was online.

I sighed and started typing. What do you want Sam?

He replied almost instantly. YOU!

My eyes widened. I stared at the screen, not sure what to say. Then another message appeared.

Can I come over?

Sam: Can I come over?

I froze. What? I hadn't seen this man in years. We'd finally reached a good place—friends, maybe even peace.

NO! Goodnight Sam.

. Good night.

I logged out so he'd see I wasn't available, then closed the laptop and headed to my bedroom. "The nerve of him," I muttered as I searched through my closet for my African attire for church. I didn't have time for Sam—not tonight. My baby was saying her poem tomorrow.

I laid out my outfit and shoes for the morning, then ran a hot bubble bath. I turned on the radio to some smooth jazz, letting the music fill the room. I tried not to think about Sam, but it was hard.

I still loved him.

As I soaked, memories of us came flooding back—the laughter, the late nights, the way he used to look at me. The good started to outweigh the bad in my mind. I stayed in the tub so long that my skin wrinkled before I finally got out.

Later, lying in bed, my thoughts wouldn't settle. It had been over ten years since my divorce from Marquee. I hadn't been with anyone since. Ours was a marriage that never should have happened.

I had gone back to church then, where they preached that shacking up meant living in sin. So we got married. I didn't want to go against the word of God.

Back then, the kids had kept me busy. Now they were grown, with lives of their own—and the quiet left too much room for memory.

I stared up at the ceiling. "Lord, why now?" I whispered. "You sustained me all these years, and I never even wanted to be with a man again. So why are these feelings coming back?"

I closed my eyes, and after a while, sleep finally came.

A few days later, I took Myiah with me to the beauty shop. Sam's sister, Kysha, has been my beautician for years, and it was time for another perm.

"Hey y'all!" she said as we walked in.

"Hey, Aunt Kysha, look!" Myiah said, hurrying toward her with my phone in hand. She was excited to show the video I'd taken of her reciting her poem at church.

"Is that you?" Kysha asked, smiling.

"Yes, ma'am!"

"You did a good job!" Kysha said proudly. "Hey y'all, this the niece I was telling y'all about—the one who's been reading since she was two years old."

"How old are you, baby?" one of the ladies asked.

"I'm three—but I'm gonna be four next month," Myiah said, holding up four fingers.

"This baby is so smart," another woman said.

Kysha leaned in close to me and whispered, "Hey girl, you know my brother here."

My heart skipped. "Where?" I asked, trying to sound casual but already glancing around.

"He's in the back, cutting somebody's hair," she said, smiling like she knew something I didn't want to admit.

"Oh," I said softly, settling into my chair. My nerves started to tingle.

Kysha looked over at me. "You not gonna go back there and speak to him?"

I shook my head. "No." Truth was, I was too nervous. I'd seen Sam plenty of times before, but after that conversation the other night—after he said 'You'—I couldn't shake the feeling it stirred up.

"Thanks for your business, man. I'll see you in two weeks."

It was his voice. Sam was walking down the hall with his client. He glanced over his shoulder into Kysha's suite—and then stopped. His eyes landed right on me, sitting in the chair, Myiah beside me with her books.

He did a double take. "Oh snap—look who it is," he said, walking straight toward me.

My heart started pounding.

"My girl," he said as he leaned down, his scent catching me off guard. He smelled so good I had to close my eyes for a second, just taking it in.

Then he reached past me and scooped Myiah into his arms. "Ahh, I gotcha!" he said, tickling her as she giggled. After a moment, he set her back down and turned his attention to me.

"Hey, Miss Ma'am," he said, looking right into my eyes.

Everyone in the shop went quiet, watching us like it was a scene from a movie.

"Why'd you get offline last night without responding?" he asked.

I could feel my cheeks burning. "Umm… don't you have a client's hair to finish?" I said, avoiding his question.

He chuckled. "You right. I got two more clients. Come see me when Kysha's done with your hair."

Before walking out, he leaned over to his sister. "I'll pay for her hair—just let me know how much." Then he looked back at me, winked, and walked out.

The whole shop erupted. "Okay, girl! You still got it!" one of the ladies said.

I just looked up at the little TV on the wall, pretending not to hear them. I could see Kysha walking toward me, grinning.

"Girllll," she said, playfully pushing my shoulder. "What's going on there?"

"Nothing at all," I said, smiling without taking my eyes off the screen.

"Uh-huh," she said with a laugh, shaking her head as she walked back to her client.

"Oh my, you did that, girl!" I said to Kysha, staring at myself in the mirror and admiring her work.

"You look pretty, Maw-Maw," Myiah said, glancing up from where she was playing with one of her aunt's mannequin heads, brushing its hair.

"Thank you, baby. You ready to go?"

"Hold up," Kysha said, placing a hand on my shoulder. "You not gonna go see your baby daddy?" she asked playfully.

I laughed nervously. I was planning to sneak out and avoid him, I thought to myself.

"I guess," I said hesitantly, looking up at her. "Can you watch her for me?"

"Yeah, little mama's fine right here," she said, handing Myiah some rollers to play with.

I took a deep breath and started walking toward the back of the shop—to the small suite Kysha let her brother use from time to time. When I peeked around the doorway, he was standing in front of the mirror, cleaning his clippers and blades.

He looked up, caught my reflection in the mirror, and smiled.

"Why you peeping around the door? Come in," he said.

I stepped inside slowly.

"Dang, you look good," he said, his eyes trailing over me. "Kysha did a good job on you too."

"Thanks," I said quietly, feeling my heart start to race. I moved toward one of the chairs and sat down. "Why'd you pay for my hair? And why'd you want me to come see you before I left?"

He walked over, sat beside me, and took my hands in his. His voice softened.

"I know I've said I'm sorry before…" He paused, looking down, then back up into my eyes. "But I love you. And I miss you."

The words sent chills through me. No matter how much time had passed, this man still had my heart. For a moment, all the hurt and pain disappeared. I sat there quietly, trying to hold back tears. Those were the words I'd waited years to hear.

I stood up. "Sam, I have to drop Myiah back off at Shay's," I said, turning my face away so he wouldn't see the emotion written all over it.

He stood too, reached out, and gently grabbed my arm to stop me. Then he pulled me close, wrapping his arms around me.

"Don't go," he whispered.

I closed my eyes and gave in, wrapping my arms around him.
   Oh, how I love this man.
   I broke free from his loving embrace, his cologne still lingering on my shirt. I turned to walk away, but stopped at the door.
   "Give me your phone," I said, turning back to face him.
   He walked over to his station, grabbed his phone, and handed it to me. I started typing. Then my phone rang.
   "Here," I said, handing it back. "Now you have my number. Call me tomorrow."
   And he did—every day since.

Ding. My phone buzzed — a message. It was Sam: What are you doing?

I texted back, Just watching TV. About to go in the kitchen and fix me something to eat.

He replied, Okay, I'm on my way. Have me a plate ready too.

I smiled and sent him a smiling emoji. We'd been seeing each other for a while now; he'd practically moved in. Looking around the apartment, I noticed his things scattered everywhere — his shoes by the couch, a jacket draped over the chair.

I headed to the kitchen and took out everything I needed to make my famous stuffed chicken — his favorite. I turned on some music and started cooking, something I genuinely loved doing.

A little while later, there was a knock at the door. He's here.

When I opened it, he asked, "Hey, why was the deadbolt on?"

I froze for a second — I'd forgotten he had one of my spare keys. "It's just a habit," I said, closing the door behind him.

He walked straight to the kitchen. "Smells good in here," he said, lifting the lids off the pots. "You made a pineapple upside-down cake too?" His voice lit up with excitement.

"You ready to eat?" I asked, smiling from ear to ear.

I fixed our plates — double portions for him, since he loved to eat — and we sat in front of the TV, enjoying the food and a movie.

Afterward, Sam excused himself to the back. He was gone for a while, and when he came back, he looked anxious. His eyes were wide, but I didn't think much of it.

He walked up to me, kissing my neck as his hands slid down to unbutton my pants. Our lovemaking was more intense than usual — raw, passionate, and so good. It started in the living room and ended in the bedroom.

Afterwards, we lay there in silence, and then he blurted out, "Marry me."

19

Chapter 19

Silent Regrets

The next morning, I woke up to the smell of bacon. I lay in bed, staring at the ceiling, thinking about what happened last night. My thoughts were all over the place. Then I heard off-key singing coming from the kitchen, and I couldn't help but smile.

I grabbed a pillow, hugged it tight, and closed my eyes. I wanted this so badly. Is this real? I pressed my nose against the pillow, breathing in the faint scent of him that still lingered.

Just as I started to get up, Sam walked in carrying a tray of breakfast — even with a little flower on it.

"Get back in bed," he said, smiling as he approached.

"Aww, thank you," I said, pulling the blankets back over my legs.

He set the tray in front of me. "Don't start yet. Let me go get mine."

I watched him dance out of the room, my heart full from the love he was showing me. When he came back, he climbed into bed with his own tray, and we ate together, laughing and teasing each other between bites.

Later that day, I had a hair appointment with his sister, Kysha. When she was finishing up, Sam came in. I stood in front of the mirror, admiring my hair, when he walked over and said, "Here," slipping a ring onto my finger.

Here? I thought.

In the moment, I pretended to be overjoyed, trying not to let him — or everyone else watching — see my disappointment. The ring was already fading on the inside, and I was pretty sure the diamonds weren't real.

I looked at him and forced a smile as his sister and the others shouted, "Congratulations!" I felt both excited and mortified.

Kysha playfully hit him on the arm. "Boy, you play too much. Did you even ask her right?"

"I already did all that," he said.

I think she could tell I wasn't too happy about the way he did it, but she smiled and pretended right along with me.

Things started moving fast. His sister, Kysha, jumped right in to help plan the wedding. Doing hair wasn't her only talent — she was also an event planner. Invitations went out, engagement photos were done. I spent so much money, though not nearly as much as some weddings I'd heard about.

My friend Regina agreed to cater, and her food was always on point.

I glanced down at my hand, admiring the ring that now sat there. My mind drifted back to the night Sam's baby sister came over with these beautiful rings, presenting them to her brother to give to me. I just love his family, I thought.

But Sam had changed a lot since we moved in together. I'd taken on most of the responsibility for planning the wedding, and we hadn't been spending as much time together. I'd picked up extra hours at work to help cover wedding expenses and household bills, while he'd been hanging out more with his friends and the Mason group he'd joined.

I wished he would stop trying to play drug dealer and get a real job, but every time I brought it up, it turned into a fight. So I just let him be.

Beep.

I heard a phone go off.

Beep. There it was again.

I searched the living room where the sound came from. Sam wasn't home — I was alone. Finally, I found it tucked between the couch cushions.

It was locked. I tried a few combinations, then entered Sam's birthday. Ding. It opened.

My stomach dropped. There were messages from several women on an app called Plenty of Fish, asking him to come over — again. Again? My heart started to race as I scrolled through the messages and pictures.

There were texts of him asking women for nude photos — and them sending them. But the most shocking message was from a woman demanding he return her ring and other jewelry he'd stolen after they had sex. The date was around the same time he'd given me that faded ring.

Tears spilled down my face. I couldn't believe this was happening again.

Then I opened one of the videos in his gallery. It showed a woman who looked dazed — and a man having sex with her from behind. I dropped the phone.

In my heart, I knew that man was Sam.

I sat on the couch in the dark, crying — I couldn't believe this was happening to me. I had put my trust in this man again.

Before getting back with Sam, I'd even sat down with my kids and asked if they were okay with it. Even though he was their father, he was never really there for them, and I knew that could reopen old wounds. They all said the same thing — if I was happy, that's what mattered.

The door opened. Sam stumbled in, drunk and high. High on what, I couldn't tell.

"Why you sitting in the dark?" he asked, flipping on the lights.

I was sitting there, holding what I now called his secret phone in my hand.

"Here," I said, tossing it at him. "Your phone's been going off. You might want to answer your text messages."

I stood and started toward the bedroom, but he grabbed my arm.

"What are you talking about?" he demanded. "That's not mine."

"Do you think I'm stupid?" I snapped, pulling free.

He grabbed me again, trying to explain, saying all that stuff was "old news." I didn't want to hear it. I twisted and pulled, trying to get out of his grip, but he held tight. Then, suddenly, he tried to turn it on me — like I was the problem.

I stared at him, stunned, then yanked my arm away. He stumbled and fell back onto the couch.

Without another word, I went to the bedroom. He didn't follow. He just stayed there, passed out the same way he'd fallen.

The next morning, I was supposed to meet my daughters and some friends for brunch. I'd told everyone I didn't want a bachelorette party — this was my second marriage — but they insisted on doing something, so brunch was the compromise.

As I walked past Sam, still passed out on the couch, anger and heartbreak twisted inside me. I wanted to cancel, to crawl back into bed and disappear. But instead, I did what I always do — put on a smile and pretend everything's fine.

I grabbed my purse, headed for the door, and slammed it behind me, hoping the sound would wake him up.

The place where we met up was beautifully decorated by my daughters, and the food was absolutely exquisite. When it was time, I stood to give a brief speech.

"Thank you all for coming out and celebrating me. It means the world to have so much love surrounding me," I said.

As I spoke, I began to get teary-eyed—not just from the love in the room, but from the thoughts swirling in my mind about what happened last night between Sam and me. Who am I really marrying? I wondered. Does he love me like he says he does, or is it all just for show?

The questions kept racing through my head, making it hard to fully enjoy the moment. Sam had burned so many bridges, especially with his own family. Was this his way of trying to get back in their good graces—pretending to be someone he's not?

My phone rang for the sixth time.

"Dang, Momma," Ashley said. "Somebody's really trying to get in touch with you. They've been blowing your phone up."

"It's your dad," I sighed. "But I'm not trying to talk to him right now. Today is about me—spending time with my girls and everyone in this room."

I forced a smile. "Now pass me another slice of cake," I said, trying to hide the sadness behind it.

When the brunch was over, I got in my car, dreading the thought of going home. Instead, I took a detour to the park—the place I'd go when I needed to be alone, to think, and to talk to the Lord.

I didn't even get out of the car. I just sat there, closed my eyes, and took a deep breath. For a moment, peace washed over me.

Then—ring, ring. The sound shattered my quiet.

"Hello?" I answered. "Sam, what is it?"

"Where are you?" he yelled through the phone.

"Why?" I said, trying to sound calm, maybe even a little uninterested.

"Don't play with me, where ar—"

I cut him off. "I'll be home in a minute." I hung up before he could say another word.

How dare he raise his voice at me! I thought, anger bubbling up. I'm so sick of this.

Tears started to fall as I sat there, crying and praying. "Why, God? Why?"

Finally, I drove home, bracing myself for whatever scene I was about to walk into. I pulled up to the house and sat there for a moment, staring at the door, afraid of what waited behind it.

When I walked inside, Sam was at the table—elbows resting on the surface, hands clasped together, chin propped on top. His eyes followed me.

"I'm only going to ask you once," he said, voice low and hard. "Where have you been?"

I rolled my eyes and sighed. "The girls threw me a little party to celebrate our happy day," I said, my voice dripping with sarcasm. "I'm tired. I'm going to bed."

As I turned to walk away, his chair screeched across the floor and slammed over. He stormed after me.

"This conversation isn't over!" he shouted.

"Oh yeah?" I spun around to face him. "Then let's talk about your secret phone—the one with the naked pictures and your dick! Yeah, let's talk about that!"

His face drained of color.

"What are you talking about?" he stammered.

"Oh, now you want to play stupid?" I said. "Sam, just leave me alone."

Tears streamed down my cheeks as I turned toward the bedroom, leaving him standing there in shock—or maybe just too drunk to remember what happened last night. Either way, I didn't care.

I just wanted to go to bed.

A short while later, Sam came into the room. I was already in bed, facing the wall, trying to avoid any more conversation. I clenched my chest, holding back tears, thinking, I just can't take any more hurt.

Sam undressed quietly and climbed into bed beside me. He slipped his arm around my waist, pulling me closer. His breath brushed against my ear as he whispered, "I'm sorry for hurting you. That stuff is old—it's behind me. I love you."

He pulled me in tighter. The tears I'd been holding back finally fell, harder this time. My heart wanted to believe every word he said, but my mind kept replaying everything I'd seen on that phone.

So I just closed my eyes and tried to drift off to sleep in his arms—confused, torn, and still aching inside.

20

Chapter 20

Silent Thoughts of Escape

"Ah, this rain—why today?" I muttered as I drove, trying to make it to the church early, just in case Kysha needed help with anything before the wedding started.

The night before, me and my girls had been busy ironing tablecloths, getting every wrinkle out, and helping with whatever jobs she needed done.

When I pulled up to the church, a few of the helpers were arriving too. I started unpacking my car when someone came rushing over.

"No ma'am, this is your day," one of the ladies said, grabbing the things from my hands. She gently took charge, escorting me toward the room set up for the bridal party.

I tried sneaking off to peek at the ceremony room to see if they needed help, but mostly because I was dying to see how everything looked. But my escort stopped me.

"Strict orders," she said with a smile. "You're not allowed to see it until you walk down the aisle. Kysha wants it to be a surprise."

When I finally reached the bridal suite, nerves started to kick in. My dress hung on the door, shimmering under the soft light, and I just stood there for a moment in awe.

Then my maid of honor walked in. "You ready for this?" she asked, wrapping me in a hug.

"Yeah..." I said, though my voice didn't sound nearly as confident as I wanted it to.

Right behind her came my daughters—and my two little flower girls, my beautiful, excited granddaughters.

"You girls ready? Have you been practicing?" I asked.

"Yes ma'am!" they both chimed, showing off how they planned to walk and toss their rose petals.

"Great job! High five," I said, laughing as they reached up to slap my hand.

"Have you guys seen the room yet?" I asked, eager to know how it was coming along.

"Yeah, it's looking good," Ashley said with a reassuring smile. "It's gonna be real nice, Momma. Don't worry."

A loud clap of thunder erupted, and fear washed over my face. What if no one shows up because of the rain? What if this is a sign? What if—

Before I could spiral further, Cristina, my maid of honor, noticed the look on my face. She took my hands and said gently, "Stop worrying. Everything's going to be okay."

Someone else chimed in, "You know, when it rains on your wedding day, it means good luck."

Good luck, I thought to myself. I need all the luck I can get right now—my faith feels a little shaky.

Time felt strange—moving fast and slow all at once. The photographer was snapping pictures of everything: me getting my makeup done, fixing my hair, even my shoes.

When everyone was finally dressed, I slipped into my gown. The room filled with soft gasps and "You look beautiful!" My daughters teared up as they hugged me.

Then my mother and mother-in-law entered. We joined hands in a circle for prayer, and the photographer captured the moment.

As we finished, my mother-in-law leaned close and whispered in my ear, "You know, you don't have to marry him. You're already one of my daughters."

We both laughed softly.

Guests started to arrive, and the rain had stopped. Maybe things are turning around, I thought.

Then someone said, "That fool's out there doing a wardrobe change!"

Sam was outside mingling with the guests, laughing and joking, being his usual outspoken self. He hadn't come home the night before—he'd stayed at his family's BBQ shop, preparing the meat for the reception with one of his friends.

I could hear him now in the hallway. Something about his energy felt off—he seemed overly hyped.

The wedding was running behind schedule. I was getting anxious, and I could sense the guests were too. Family and friends from out of town were waiting for me to walk down the aisle.

Then I heard, "Places, everyone!"

One by one, the wedding party lined up. The doors opened, and they began walking down the aisle. Sam's baby sister made sure I was picture-perfect before taking her place.

I couldn't see the ceremony space yet—I was around the corner, waiting for my cue.

Then the flower girls entered, tossing rose petals for me to walk on.

The doors closed again. My son appeared at my side, offering his arm. My heart started pounding.

Then I heard our song begin to play. The doors opened. Everyone stood.

As we stepped forward, tears welled up in my eyes. The room was breathtaking—everything turned out beautifully. I could feel the love radiating from every person there. Not everyone had been able to make it, but you couldn't tell by the crowd that filled the room.

My son looked at me and asked, "You ready?"

I took a shaky breath, looked back at him nervously, and said, "Yes."

We began to walk down the aisle — all eyes on us, cameras flashing. You could hear soft awws echoing through the room. My stomach was in knots. My body trembled as I tried not to cry, but tears slipped free with every step I took toward the altar.

One of the ladies helping Kysha coordinate the wedding pressed a tissue into my hand before I started walking. I pulled it out and gently dabbed the tears forming in my eyes, careful not to smear my makeup.

When I looked up, there was Sam — standing by the pastor, looking so handsome. He caught my eye, and I could tell he was trying to hold himself together.

When we reached the stage, the pastor asked, "Who giveth this woman away?"
"My handsome son said proudly, "I do."

I took Sam's hand, and it was time for the prayer. But Sam wouldn't stop acting silly — cracking jokes, fidgeting, refusing to be serious. I squeezed his hand as hard as I could, silently pleading with him to stop.

Finally, the pastor paused and said firmly that this was a serious moment and needed to be treated as such. I wanted to sink into the floor. Embarrassment burned through me. As I stood there, fighting back tears, a thought crept in — Is this how our whole marriage is going to be?

I had waited for this day for so long. Yet, right then, all I wanted was to run — to bolt through those doors just behind Sam. They're right there, I thought. Just go. But my body didn't move.

Instead, I kept frowning, squeezing his hand every time he started clowning around. Even the kiss — he turned that into a joke. I smiled like I wasn't hurt, but inside, my heart sank.

As we walked down the aisle together, he danced playfully around me, still making a show of everything. I smiled for the cameras, but I was ready for it all to be over.

At the reception, I moved from table to table, speaking with guests and posing for photos. One of my friends said, "Sam is a whole show by himself — he had us laughing the entire time."

An uneasy feeling washed over me. I forced a polite smile, though what I really wanted to do was scream.

His sister overheard and pulled me aside. "You know he acts like that when he's nervous," she said softly. "That's just how he copes."

I smiled at her, but inside I thought, That doesn't make it right. This was supposed to be a special day. Couldn't he be serious, just once?

When I looked back across the room, Sam was still bouncing around, full of energy. I shook my head, the thought crossing my mind — He's got to be high. This is how he was acting when I picked him up from one of his friend's house and I found that little blue bag in his jean pocket. And he swore he wasn't using just selling.

As the reception came to an end, Sam, a few friends, and I stayed behind to help his sister pack up.

"There are extra pans of food back here," someone said.

I remembered my maid of honor, Christina, was throwing a birthday party for her sister-in-law, so we decided to take the extra food over there.

As soon as we arrived, Sam's phone rang. It was his Mason brother.

"Yeah, sure, come over here," Sam said into the phone.

I looked at him in disbelief. How are you going to invite someone over to someone else's house? I thought.

He caught the look on my face but kept talking as he walked outside toward the truck. I followed him.

"Where are you going?" I asked.

"I'll be back," he said quickly. "Go back in there with your homegirl. I'm about to make some money. I'll be back in a minute."

Make some money? Are you kidding me? I thought, fuming.

I walked back into the house, trying to stay calm, but minutes turned into nearly an hour. We were only supposed to be there for a short while. By the time he finally showed back up—with his friends—I was furious.

"Take me home. Now," I said, my voice shaking with anger.

Sam looked at me like he hadn't done a single thing wrong.

"We'll go in a minute," he said. "The fellas wanted to make a plate."

He reached for me, trying to hug me so I wouldn't make a scene in front of his Mason brothers, but I pulled away. I stormed out, opened the truck door, and climbed in.

I sat there in silence until he was finally ready to leave. I was over everything.

Over the next few days, Sam tried to make up for everything he thought I was mad about—but he never truly took accountability for any of it.

When the photographer finally sent over the wedding photos and video, everything looked beautiful. For a moment, I almost forgot how I'd felt that day.

Then I saw it—the part at the altar where he was playing around. My heart broke all over again.

I watched with tears in my eyes, asking myself why I didn't just run through those doors when I had the chance.

I stopped the video and closed my laptop. I couldn't watch anymore. All I could think about was the money I'd spent on a day that was supposed to be so special—for both of us.

21

Chapter 21

Silent Storm

I sat by the window, watching the empty driveway, my eyes flicking to the clock every few seconds. Each minute that passed felt like a punch in my stomach. He's late again.

I pressed my forehead against the cool glass and exhaled, fogging up the pane. The silence in the house felt heavy, like it was holding its breath with me. I'm going to be late again, I whispered to myself.

I pushed away from the window and walked down the hall, my tennis shoes squeaked against the floor. I really thought things would be different once we got married. It had been over a year, and still, nothing had changed.

I prayed every night—sometimes out loud, sometimes in the quiet of my thoughts—but the answers never came. I did everything I'd been taught a good wife should do. Maybe more than I should have. Some would probably call it foolish.

I stopped at the hallway mirror and studied my reflection. The woman staring back at me looked tired—eyes puffy from tears I thought I'd hidden well. I dabbed concealer around the corners of my eyes, forcing a small smile that didn't reach my face.

Then, the front door creaked open.

"Finally," I muttered, grabbing my work bag and hurrying toward the entryway.

Sam stood in the doorway, his expression unreadable, eyes fixed on me.

"Where do you think you're going with all that makeup on?" he asked, his voice sharp, his lips curling into a smirk. "Who are you trying to look good for?"

My heart sank. "Sam, please," I said, reaching for the keys in his hand. "I'm already late. I just need to go."

He raised the keys just out of reach, teasingly. "No," he said, his tone low, controlling. "I'll take you."

He turned toward the door and gestured for me to go ahead.

I hesitated for a second, staring at him. My chest felt tight, but I was too tired to argue.

So I just walked through the door.

I sat in the car, staring out the window and trying not to look bothered as Sam drove wildly, switching lanes and cutting cars off. My hand clenched the door handle while I thought about all the cars Sam had wrecked in the past year with his reckless driving.

"I know I'm going to be late, Sam, but could you please slow down?" I said, watching how fast he was going and how close we were to the car in front of us.

My body jerked forward when he slammed on the brakes. We stopped just inches away from a collision. I looked at him, anger and fear tightening my chest, but Sam only laughed and brushed it off, as if nothing was wrong.

When we finally pulled up to my job, I had never been so relieved to see the building—anything to get out of that car. I opened the door and started to step out, but Sam grabbed my arm and yanked me back toward him.

"You're not gonna give me a kiss? Oh, you must have some man in there you don't want me to see," he said.

I stared at him, confused. Where did that come from?

"No. What are you talking about?" I said, looking him straight in the face.

"It better not be," he muttered, leaning in to kiss me. His breath reeked of liquor. I forced a small grin to hide the concern rising inside me as I stepped out of the car. He stayed parked, watching me walk into the building, as if waiting to catch me doing something wrong.

A couple of hours passed before my phone rang again—for the third time since I'd been at work. I glanced at the screen and sighed. Of course. Sam. Right on cue.

"Hello. What is it, Sam?" I answered.

"What are you doing?" he asked.

"You know I'm at work. I'm working," I said, my frustration slipping through.

"Oh really?" he replied. "Then why does your location say you're at the hotel near your job?"

"What? Please stop. I don't have time for this," I said.

The moment the words left my mouth, a FaceTime request popped up.

"Accept it," he snapped.

I paused, staring at my phone. "Sam, I'm really at work."

"Shauntilia, if you don't answer, I will come up there. Don't play with me," he said forcefully.

I accepted the call, only to reassure him. "Are you happy now? This is ridiculous."

"Let me see around your desk," he said. "I know I heard a man's voice earlier."

"You didn't. Please stop—I have to get back to work."

"Put the phone on the desk so I can see you working."

Are you kidding me? I thought.

I rolled my eyes and placed the phone on my desk. I could see him scanning the background, his eyes darting.

"Turn it a little to the left," he said, tilting his head as if he might catch something—or someone.

I tried to continue working, glancing down at my phone every so often just to appease his insecurities. I told myself that as long as I did this, he'd be fine.

I didn't realize then that he wasn't fine at all—that something much deeper was going on with him.

"Sam, go to bed. It's late—I'll see you when I get off."

"Why are you rushing me off the phone?" he said, forcing his eyes open as if he weren't already drifting to sleep.

"My phone's about to die anyway. I need to put it on the charger."

"Whatever, Shauntilia," he muttered as his face slipped off the screen. I could hear him snort.

"Don't let me catch you with that nigga," he added.

His finger fumbled across the screen, trying to end the call.

I shook my head and hung up.

I sat at my desk, staring at my computer, completely lost in thought. Is this what marriage is? I asked myself. For better or worse, huh?

I looked up at the ceiling, then closed my eyes.

"Lord," I whispered, "help me make it to the better."

Time seemed to speed up as the end of my shift approached. When it was almost time to clock out, I called Sam to make sure he was awake and downstairs waiting for me. The phone rang—no answer. I called again. Still nothing.

I gathered my things and headed for the elevators, pressing the button and thinking, He better already be down here or pulling into the parking lot by the time I reach the lobby.

He wasn't.

My exhausted body sank into one of the chairs near the sliding doors. He's not here, I thought.

"See you tomorrow," I said as my coworkers passed by one after another, heading to their cars.

"Hey girl, you need a ride?" Christina asked, stopping in front of me while digging through her purse for her keys.

"No, I'm good," I replied with a small, forced grin.

"You sure? I don't mind—I can drop you off."

I checked the time on my phone. Thirty minutes had passed, and still no Sam.

"Actually... yes. Thank you. You're a lifesaver," I said quietly. "I don't know where Sam is."

Just as we started walking toward her car, Sam came flying through the parking lot with loud music blaring. He pulled up beside us and rolled down the passenger window.

"My bad—I know," he said casually, turning the music down and greeting Christina.

The embarrassment washed over me, heavy and suffocating. The smell of weed and alcohol poured out of the car, stealing my breath. I looked at Christina, shame burning in my eyes.

Me. The good girl. The church girl. The one always praying—married to a man who drank and smoked.

She saw the hurt immediately. Christina stepped closer, wrapped her arms around me, and whispered the words I desperately needed.

"It's going to be okay. I'm praying for you. You keep praying too—things will turn around. I'll see you tomorrow."

Tears welled up, but I forced them back. I didn't want Sam to see me cry.

"Okay. See you tomorrow," I said softly.

I opened the car door and got in. Sam leaned over to kiss me, but I turned my head toward the window and closed my eyes.

"Just drive."

22

Chapter 22

Silent Plea

Sam pulled up to the house, and I reached for the door handle, ready to escape the tension that had filled the car ride home. My body ached from working all night. I grabbed my bag and headed toward the front door.

Sam hesitated. Something had caught his eye across the parking lot—a blue car parked two buildings down. He took a picture of it, then looked at me with a frown and shook his head. I glanced at him, confused, while digging through my bag for my keys. I was too tired to try to figure out what was going on in his head.

When I walked inside, my mouth dropped open.

It looked like a tornado had torn through the place. Just twelve hours ago, I'd left a clean, clutter-free home. I have to clean this now, I thought as I picked up empty beer bottles scattered across the end table and floor. Cigarette butts littered the room, along with a small bag that held only God knows what.

Well, that explains his behavior.

Lord, please take this habit away from him.

As I finished straightening up, I realized Sam still hadn't come inside. I went to the window. He was sitting in the car, smoking.

He knows I hate that smell. Now he's smoking in the house and in my car. The disrespect was becoming too much. He used to hide it from me—now his whole attitude had changed. He smoked whenever he wanted, saying it helped keep him calm.

Well, it ain't working, I thought as I closed the curtain and headed toward the bedroom.

I pushed myself forward, searching for enough strength just to make it to the bathroom. I turned on the shower, and steam quickly filled the room. My body felt heavy. I stripped off my clothes, as if stripping away the weight of my life, and stepped under the water.

The heat wrapped around me, therapeutic against my crying body.

Ahh.

This is what I needed.

After the much-needed relaxing shower, I got into bed and began to slowly drift off to sleep. Suddenly, my covers were snatched off me. I was yanked out of bed by my hair, my body slamming hard against the floor. Sam stood over me, shouting, accusing me of talking to the person whose car he had been sitting outside, staring at.

"What are you talking about?" I cried as tears poured uncontrollably down my face. "Sam, stop! Please!" I begged as if my life depended on it, because I knew what was coming next.

In that moment, a flashback hit me. Less than a month ago, I had escaped. I was free—away from the hurt and the pain.

You had a gun, saying no one loved you, saying you were going to end your life. You acted as if I was the only one who could save you, begging and pleading for me to come back. And once again, I forgave you for hurting me.

Why did I allow this man to talk his way back into my life?

Lord, help me.

I folded myself into a ball, my head tucked between my legs, begging him to stop. I tried to reassure him, telling him it was all in his head and that I loved him. He just stood there, staring down at me, clutched on the ground.

"Shauntilia, stop playing me!" he yelled as he moved from standing over me to blocking the bedroom door. "I heard you in here talking to him, saying, 'Look at him, he ain't nothing but a dope head.'"

"Sam, what are you talking about?" I said through sobs. "My phone is literally in the living room. I laid it on the counter when I was straightening up. I haven't been talking to anyone."

Easing my sore body off the floor, I sat on the edge of the bed, praying this nightmare would end soon. Sam slammed the door shut and dared me not to come out. He went to the living room to do what he always did after accusing me and hurting me.

He cried. He played Marvin Sapp's "Never Would Have Made It" or some other slow gospel song. He talked to God, cried some more, then tried to come back into the room wanting sex. Sometimes I would go to him, sit beside him, and listen as he poured out his emotions to God—asking why God wouldn't just let him die. Sam had tried several times, but God spared his life every time.

CHAPTER 22

I looked around the bedroom at the camera he thought he was secretly hiding. Then I turned and looked at the air vent he had taped up because he believed I was communicating with the man through the vents. Tears streamed down my face.

I thought my love would be enough to change him. I thought he would eventually choose me over his addiction. Instead, he said I was the reason he used.

"Lord, why is this my life?"

I grabbed my Bible from the nightstand beside the bed. I'm a good wife. I go to church. I pray. Why is this happening to me? Every time he raised his hand to strike, I wanted to fight back, but something inside me always stopped me.

I hated that feeling.

"Father, I don't want to live like this anymore. I'm done."

I cried out to God like never before. I began rebuking the enemy and speaking life over myself. The more I called on Jesus, the more the Holy Spirit took over. I started speaking in tongues, and the Holy Spirit began revealing things to me—bringing things back to my remembrance.

In that moment, I wasn't worried about Sam anymore. I felt a peace I couldn't explain.

Afterward, I stood up and walked into the living room.

Gone.

I checked the hall closet—his things were gone. He left on his own... or rather, the Holy Spirit removed him. Even though he took my car, in that moment of silence, I felt free.

A week passed before I received a phone call.

"Hello?"

"Hi, Mrs. Taylor, this is the front office calling. An officer contacted us trying to reach you about your car. I guess they didn't have your number, so they found you through your car's registration. I have his number if you're ready."

"Hold on, let me grab something to write with."

"Uh-huh… okay… got it. Thank you so much."

"No problem, Mrs. Taylor. You have a good day."

"You too."

Feeling anxious, I sat on the couch and dialed the officer's number.

"Hello, Officer Spencer speaking."

"Yes, hi. This is Shauntilia. You were trying to reach me about my car."

"Yes, ma'am. It was found abandoned on a service road in front of a school, with the trunk up."

"What?! Oh my God!"

"The school's maintenance worker called it in and secured the trunk. I can meet you at the car to file a report."

"Yes, sir. Thank you so much."

"Okay, see you soon. Goodbye."

I couldn't believe he did this. What am I saying? Yes, I can. Typical Sam. I shook my head as I ordered an Uber.

Ten minutes away. I rushed to get dressed—sweats, a T-shirt, shoes—and headed outside to meet the driver.

When I arrived, I used my spare key, but the car wouldn't start.

I called his mom since she lived nearby.

"Have the police been there yet?" she asked.

"No, they're on their way."

"Well, tell them the car was stolen—but don't say it was Sam. Just say you don't know who took it."

What? Here we go again. His mother, still trying to protect him. I was over it.

"Okay," I said flatly. She could hear the frustration in my voice.

"It's so the insurance company can pay you," she added.

When she arrived, we put a little gas in the car—it was completely empty. It finally started, and she followed me to the gas station. As I drove, smoke suddenly began pouring from under the hood.
   I screamed—loud, raw, and fed up.

I was furious that he had let my car fall into such terrible condition. After filling up, I said goodbye to his mom and headed home, praying the entire way that I would make it back safely. Lord, help me get past all this anger, I whispered as tears began to stream down my cheeks.

My heart felt heavy with the pain of betrayal—once filled with longing for his love and his touch. All the emotions came flooding back, and I began crying uncontrollably, struggling to drive as I thought about everything I had lost because of this man. I had poured all of myself into the relationship, believing that would be enough to make him change.

Then I heard a small, gentle voice say, That was the problem. Instead of pouring into Me—praising Me, honoring Me—you put your husband before Me. You carried his burdens instead of giving them to Me.

You are My child, and I love you. You are stronger than you think.

A calm began to overtake me. I felt free. The rest of the drive home, I thanked God and loved on Him, my heart finally at peace.

23

Chapter 23

Silent No More!

Weeks passed, and my relationship with God grew stronger with every passing moment. I had hidden everything that was happening with Sam—the abuse, the fear—for so long that it was keeping me from truly living. But not anymore. The more I opened up about what was happening, the freer I felt.

At first, I was afraid of what people would say or how they would see me. Then I realized it wasn't about them—it was about my healing.

Sam began calling and texting strange, disturbing messages.

"I hear you talking about me, saying, 'Oh, he's doing drugs again. Look at him—he's a dope fiend, hahaha. I know you've got cameras everywhere watching me. STOP IT. Leave me alone!!"

I would read the messages and immediately begin praying for him. The drugs had clearly taken over his mind.

Then—boom, boom—a hard knock at my door.

I checked my Ring camera. It was him. He looked unrecognizable, as though he hadn't shaved or bathed in days.

"Open this door! I know you're in there!" he yelled.

I hadn't spoken to this man in over a month. I had blocked his calls and removed him from all social media.

"Go away, Sam!" I shouted through the door.

"Open this door!" he screamed, kicking it as he tried to break in.

"Sam, stop!"

I grabbed my phone and called the police.

"911, what's your emergency?"

"Yes—my ex-husband is trying to break into my house."

Just as I began giving my address, he broke through the door.

"Where is he?!" he shouted, storming through my home. "I know he's here—I heard him. Come out! I'm right here. You wanted to fight me, right?!"

"What are you talking about?" I asked as he came toward me.

He grabbed me by the neck and slammed me against the wall. He raised his hand, waiting for me to beg him to stop—to tell him I loved him, like I had done so many times before.

But this time was different.

As I stared into his eyes, I saw him clearly for the first time. His expression was empty, distorted—almost possessed.

I began pleading the blood of Jesus.

"I'm not afraid of you, devil!" I shouted.

Stunned, Sam struck the wall instead of me.

In that moment, I realized it wasn't Sam standing in front of me, but the enemy using him. I rebuked him and continued pleading the blood of Jesus.

He stepped back, staring at me.

"I'm not a devil," he said.

He grabbed me again, but this time I stood my ground, looked him straight in the eyes, and said, "I am NOT afraid of you, devil!"

He shoved me against the wall and walked out the door.

I immediately shut the door and wedged a chair against it. I checked the Ring camera and saw him walking back toward my house. He sat down on the steps outside my door.

Then he turned toward the camera and noticed the blue light.

He stood up, ripped the camera off the door, and sat back down.

I called his mother and told her everything—that he broke in and was now sitting outside my home.

She said, "He's coming there because he has nowhere else to go."

"I've called the police," I told her.

"Where do you live? I'll send his brother to get him."

As I was giving her my address, there was another knock at the door.

It was the police.

I opened the door and stepped aside. "Please, come in."

Sam was gone.

I told the officers everything and described what he was wearing.

"That sounds like the man we just passed sitting at the bus stop down the street," one officer said.

At that moment, my phone rang. It was his mother.

"Which street did you say you lived on?" she asked. "Oh—never mind. We see him. He's at the bus stop. We've got him."

I told the officers his mother had picked him up.

"Ma'am, do you want to press charges?" one asked.

"Yes," I said. "I do."

They took photos of my neck and arms and gave me contact information for domestic violence support.

As they left, I reflected on the goodness of God. The situation could have ended so differently. My family could have been planning a funeral.

So many women don't make it out alive when the other person has nothing left to lose.

Lord, You are faithful.

A few weeks later, I moved. I needed to be somewhere without a bus line—somewhere he couldn't easily reach me.

I sent a message to his sister: Your brother is still on my insurance until the end of the year. Please try to get him some help. I screenshot the insurance cards and sent them to her.

Sam was placed in a facility for a while, but he didn't stay as long as he needed to.

Our divorce was finalized a year later.

It's been three years since I've seen or heard from him.

Until now.

A Facebook message.

Hey...

Epilogue

What once tried to break me became the ground where my faith took root.

I lived under abuse, manipulation, and strongholds that distorted how I saw myself, others, and even God. For a long time, survival was my only goal. Freedom felt distant, and truth felt buried beneath fear and control. But God was not absent in those years—He was patient.

Step by step, I learned that healing was not about reclaiming power on my own, but about surrendering what had bound me. As I followed God's path—often uncertain, often uncomfortable—He began to dismantle what I could not. Lies lost their grip. Shame loosened. Fear no longer had the final word.

What surprised me most was that my healing was never meant to end with me. God used what I endured to refine my voice, not silence it. The very places where I was once wounded became places of testimony. Not to glorify pain—but to point to redemption.

Today, my purpose is simple and unwavering: to lead people to Christ. Not as someone who has it all figured out, but as someone who knows firsthand that freedom is real, transformation is possible, and no stronghold is stronger than God's truth.

This story does not end in what was done to me.
   It ends in who God is—and who He is still drawing others to become.